# Shri Amarnath Ji Yatra and Trail

## Photo Journal

**With a Self-realization process of Seeking Brahman, Knowing Brahman, and Being Brahman, as reflected in the Holy Rig Vedas and the Holy Upanishads, while walking on the Holy Yatra Trail.**

**Mridul Joshi**

**Library of Congress Control Number: 2026902604**

**ISBN 979-8-9930198-3-3 (hardcover)**

**ISBN 979-8-9930198-5-7 (paperback)**

**ISBN 979-8-9930198-4-0 (eBook)**

**Published by**

**Amba Bhavan Publications**

**Orlando, Florida, USA**

**Disclaimer:**

**This work is a personal devotional expression and is not intended as a scholarly or authoritative interpretation.**

**This book is a personal devotional journal of my Yatra to the Holy Cave of Shri Amarnath Ji. All reflections, interpretations, and artistic renderings express my own spiritual experience and reverent understanding, not doctrinal or authoritative statements.**

**Scriptural references are drawn from public-domain sources or paraphrased in my own words. This work is not affiliated with or endorsed by any temple board, trust, lineage, or religious institution.**

**All divine beings and sacred places mentioned are held in the highest respect. Any visual representations are devotional expressions of personal Darshan, not canonical depictions.**

Om

Shanti

Shanti

Shantih

Peace within...
peace around...
peace from beyond...

Shanti

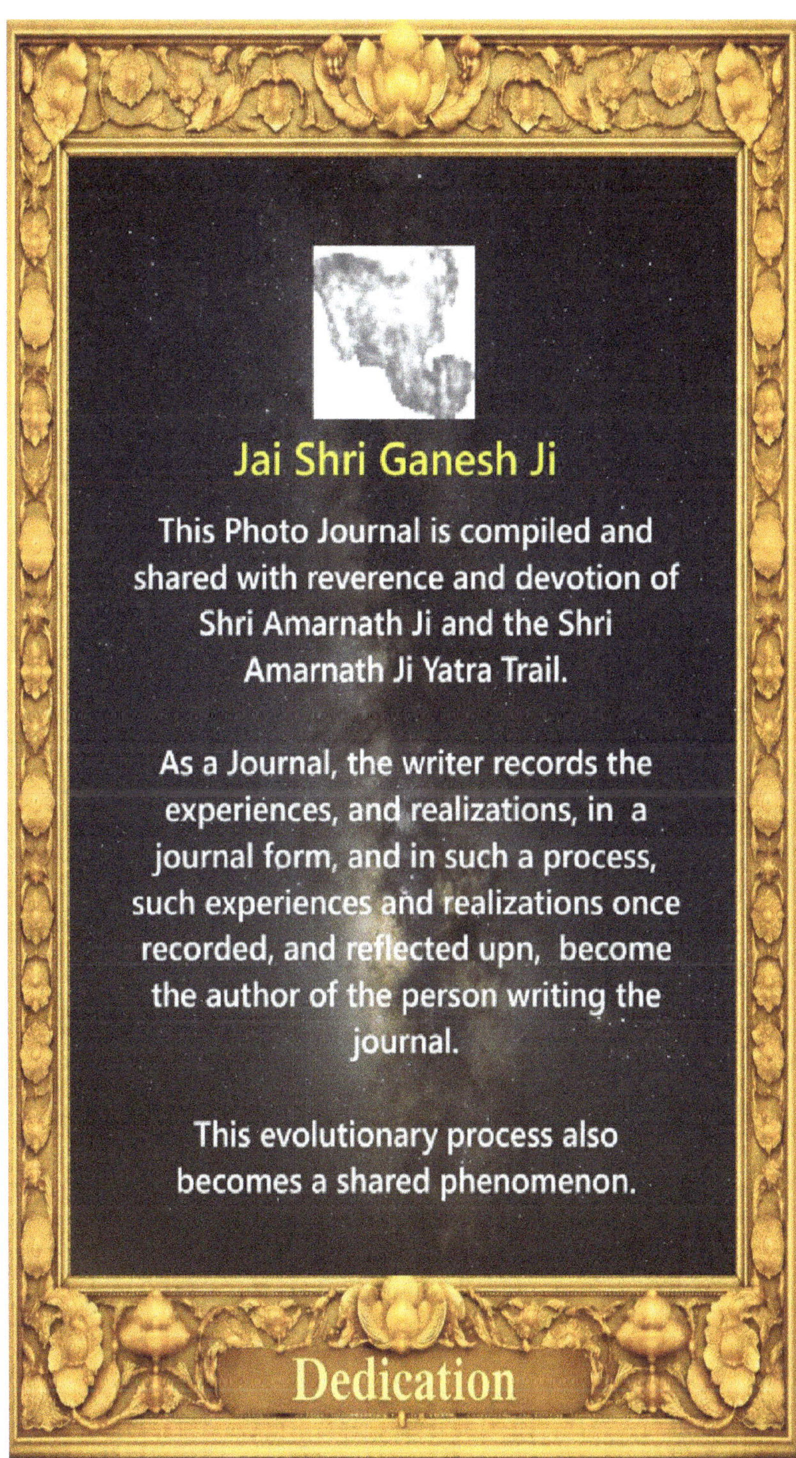
Jai Shri Ganesh Ji
This Photo Journal is compiled and shared with reverence and devotion of Shri Amarnath Ji and the Shri Amarnath Ji Yatra Trail.
As a Journal, the writer records the experiences, and realizations, in a journal form, and in such a process, such experiences and realizations once recorded, and reflected upn, become the author of the person writing the journal.
This evolutionary process also becomes a shared phenomenon.
Dedication

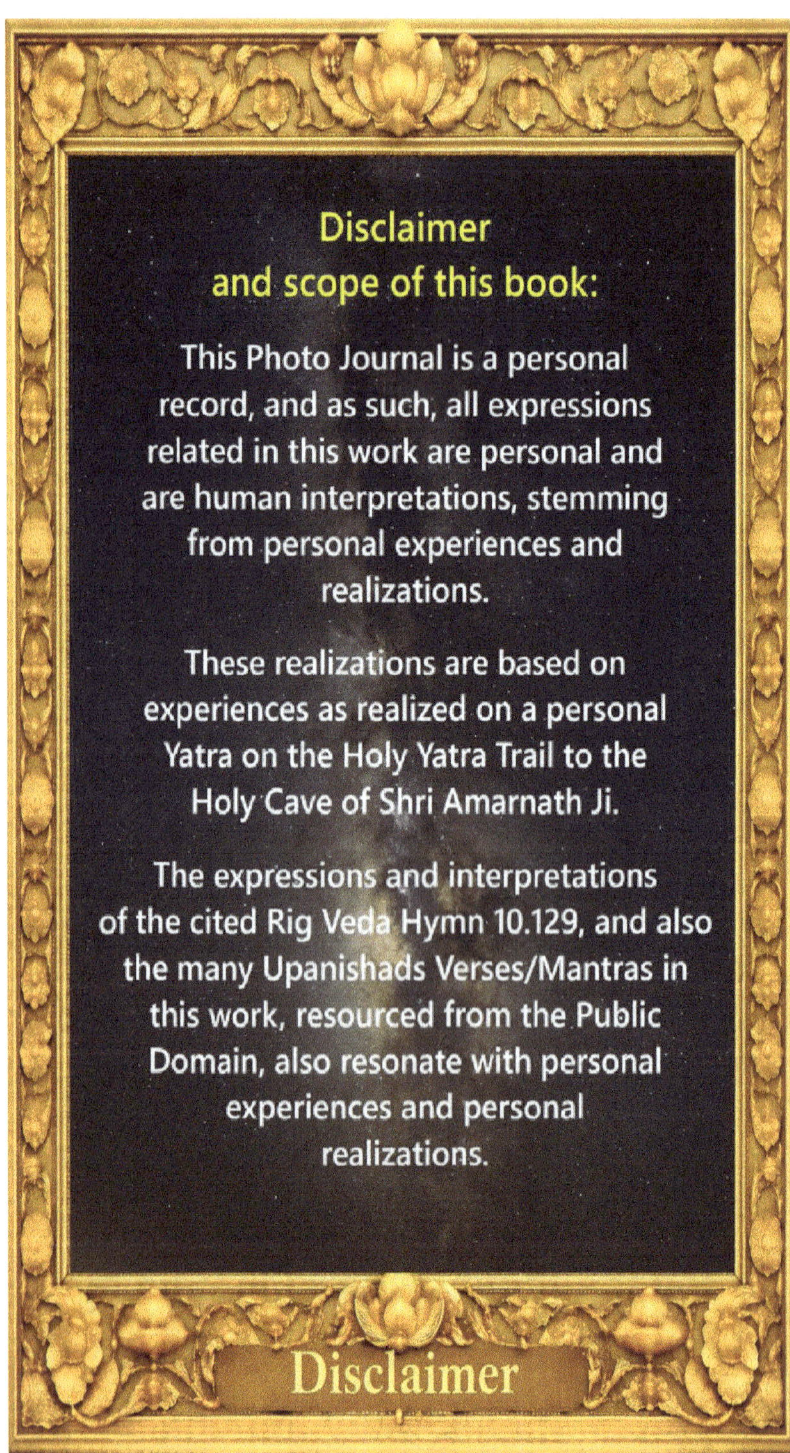
Disclaimer
and scope of this book:
This Photo Journal is a personal record, and as such, all expressions related in this work are personal and are human interpretations, stemming from personal experiences and realizations.
These realizations are based on experiences as realized on a personal Yatra on the Holy Yatra Trail to the Holy Cave of Shri Amarnath Ji.
The expressions and interpretations of the cited Rig Veda Hymn 10.129, and also the many Upanishads Verses/Mantras in this work, resourced from the Public Domain, also resonate with personal experiences and personal realizations.
Disclaimer

# Content

# DEDICATION

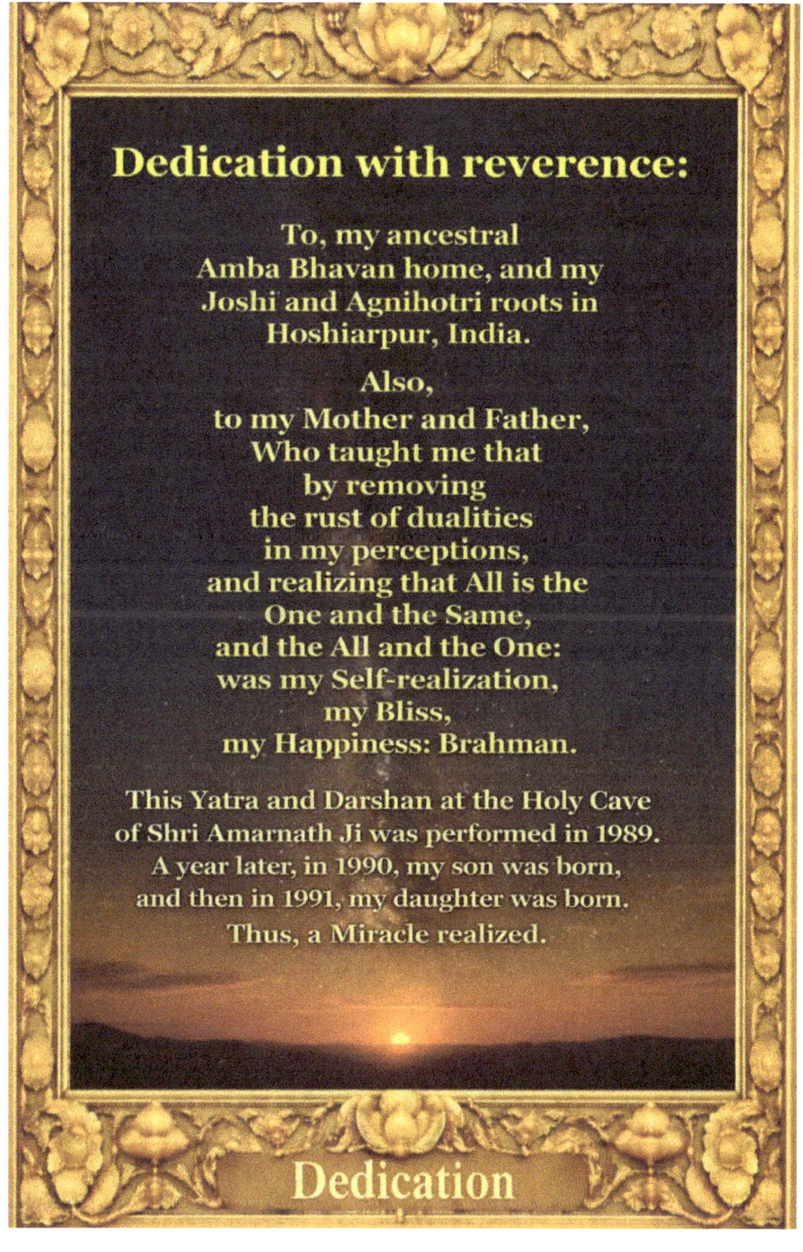

Dedication with reverence:
To, my ancestral
Amba Bhavan home, and my
Joshi and Agnihotri roots in
Hoshiarpur, India.
Also,
to my Mother and Father,
Who taught me that
by removing
the rust of dualities
in my perceptions,
and realizing that All is the
One and the Same,
and the All and the One:
was my Self-realization,
my Bliss,
my Happiness: Brahman.
This Yatra and Darshan at the Holy Cave
of Shri Amarnath Ji was performed in 1989.
A year later, in 1990, my son was born,
and then in 1991, my daughter was born.
Thus, a Miracle realized.
Dedication

# ORIGIN: RIG VEDA 10.129 NASADIYA SUKTA, AND BRAHMAN

The origin, the beginning of the present considerations are summarized as follows.

This part of the subject matter is shared based on Public Domain and commonly accepted perceptions and research and realizations, that are a present human and past human activity and are shared here as a starting point for a context and scope of this work.

Thus, in summary form Figure 1 through Figure 4, respectively, are a reduction of the research over the Public Domain of the present subject matter of interest.

**Figure 1 through 4,** respectively are 'self-evident' and are respected as a Public Domain human understanding. Thus, with this as a premise, no further elaboration is attempted and left for the reader's perspective.

This work is of a very Human Yatra, and Human realizations, and shared in reverence and devotion by a Human, on the subject of a Yatra to the Holy Cave of Shri Amarnath Ji.

The emergence of Holy Rig Veda 10.129 is estimated in the public domain as reflected in the following **Figure 1.**

**Figure 2** is a depiction of a possible Holy Rig Veda 10.129 to Brahman realization perspective view, as commonly realized in the Public Domain literature.

**Figure 3** is a two-page rendition of Rig Veda 10.129, - Hymn of Creation, Nasadiya Sukta, as an interpretation from the original text, as selected from the Public Domain.

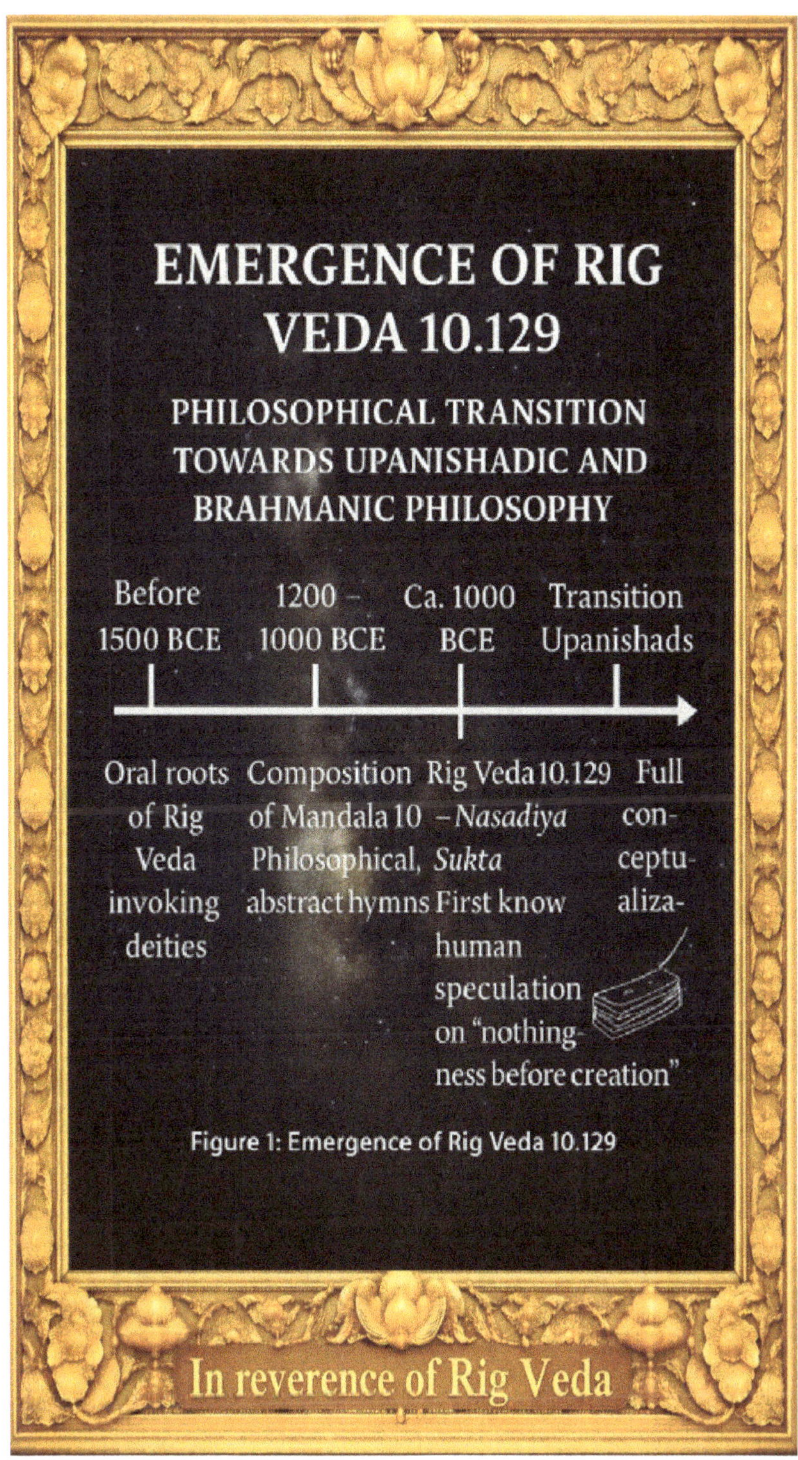


Figure 1: Emergence of Rig Veda 10.129

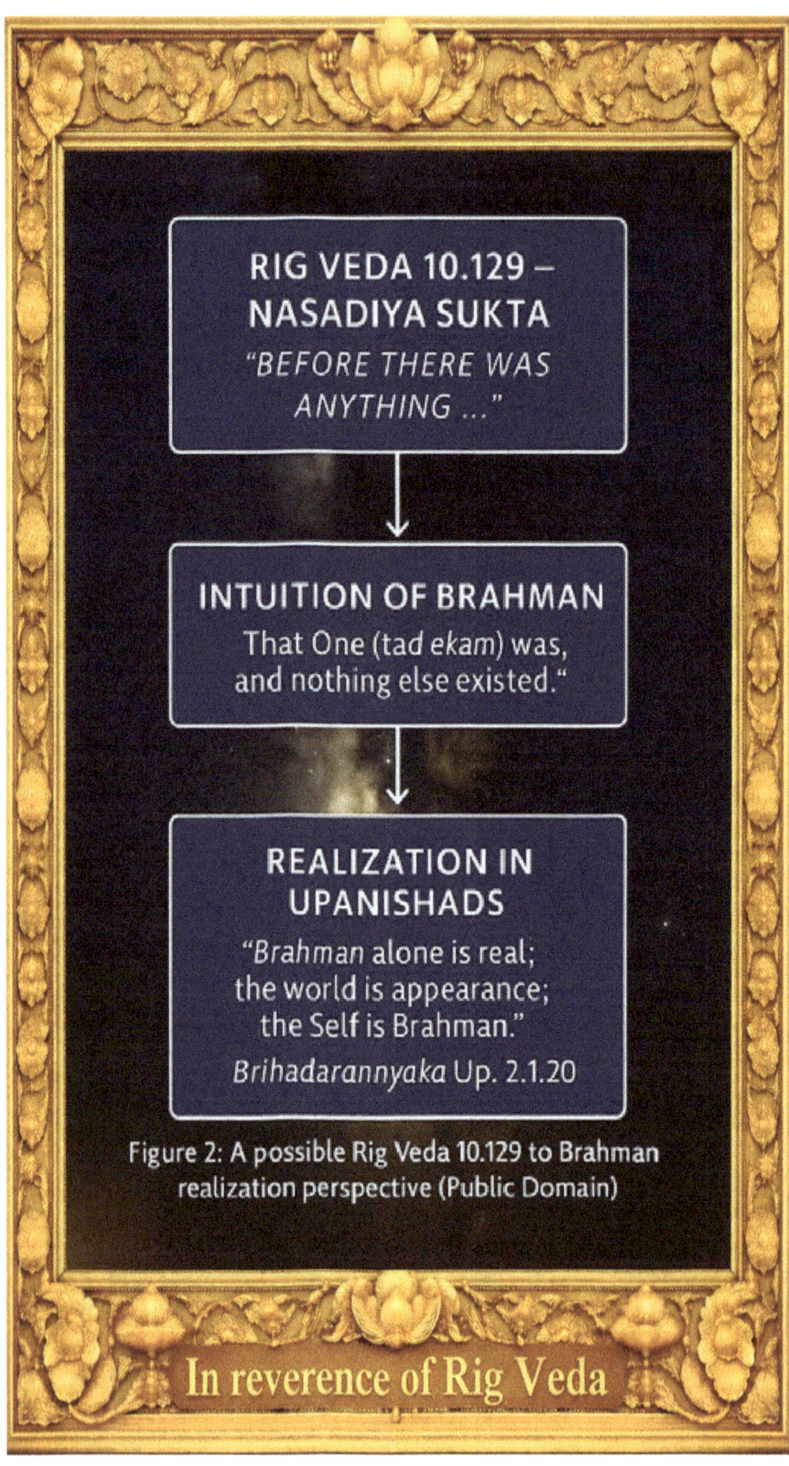
RIG VEDA 10.129 –
NASADIYA SUKTA
"BEFORE THERE WAS
ANYTHING ..."
INTUITION OF BRAHMAN
That One (tad ekam) was,
and nothing else existed."
REALIZATION IN
UPANISHADS
"Brahman alone is real;
the world is appearance;
the Self is Brahman."
Brihadarannyaka Up. 2.1.20
Figure 2: A possible Rig Veda 10.129 to Brahman
realization perspective (Public Domain)
In reverence of Rig Veda

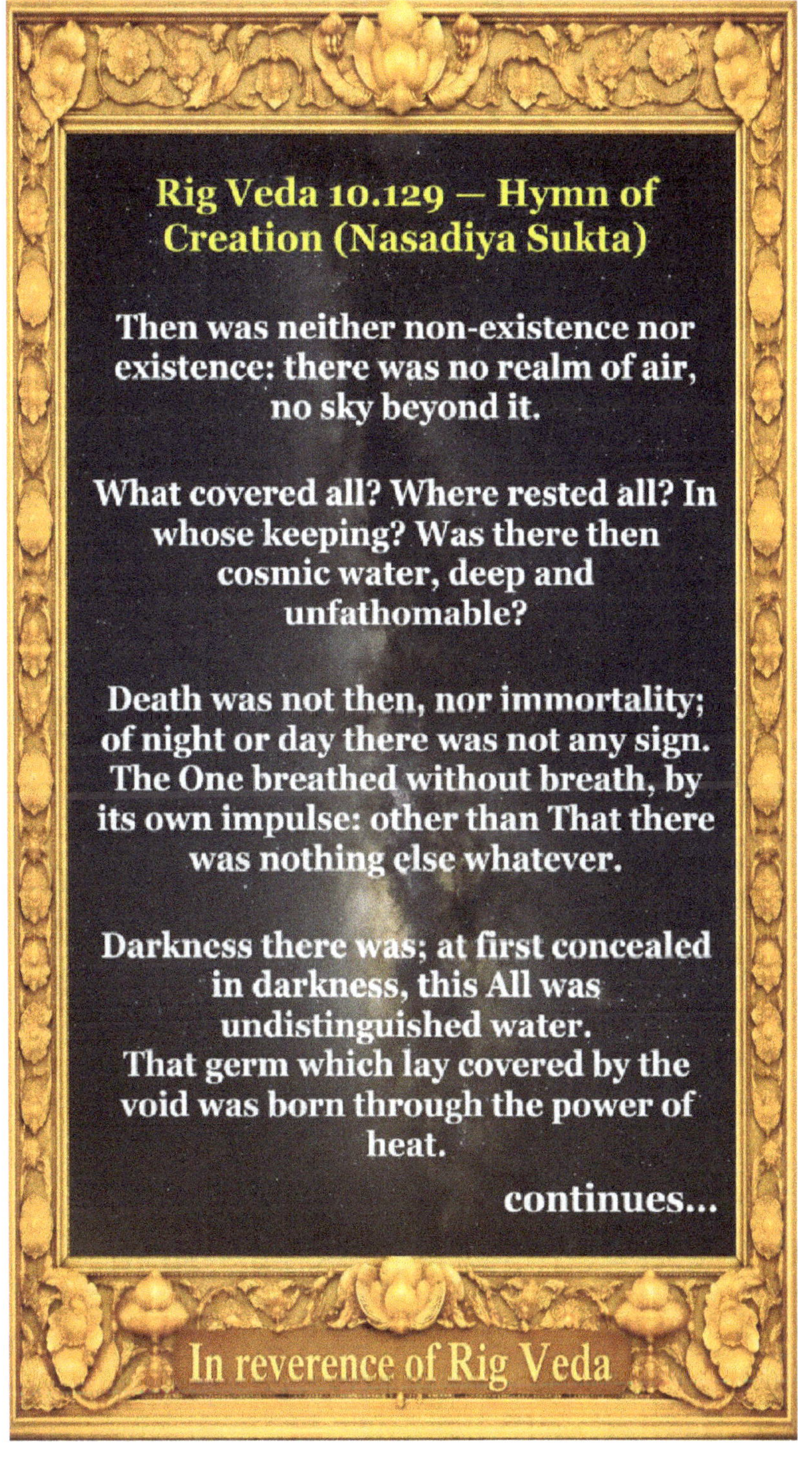
Rig Veda 10.129 – Hymn of Creation (Nasadiya Sukta)
Then was neither non-existence nor existence: there was no realm of air, no sky beyond it.
What covered all? Where rested all? In whose keeping? Was there then cosmic water, deep and unfathomable?
Death was not then, nor immortality; of night or day there was not any sign. The One breathed without breath, by its own impulse: other than That there was nothing else whatever.
Darkness there was; at first concealed in darkness, this All was undistinguished water.
That germ which lay covered by the void was born through the power of heat.
continues...
In reverence of Rig Veda

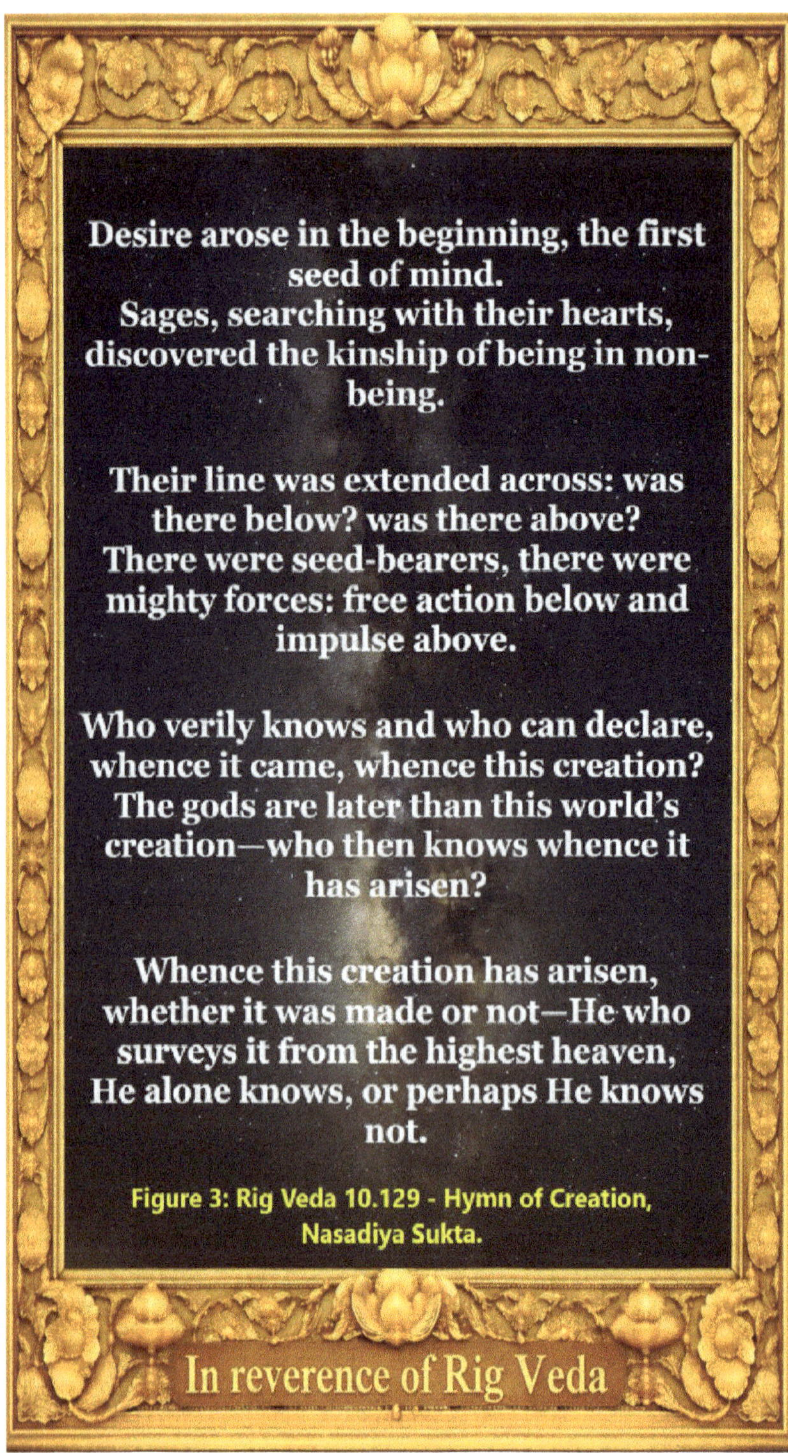


Figure 3: Rig Veda 10.129 - Hymn of Creation, Nasadiya Sukta.

## A HOMAGE TO OUR VEDIC ANCESTORS

Finally, **Figure 4** is a summary list of some of the researched Upanishads Verses that were considered for this work. Furthermore, such noted Upanishadic Verses of this compilation are further explored and realized, each respective Upanishadic Verse at a time, within the body of this work. These respective Upanishads Verses are seen to be reflective of the awareness of 'Brahman' and such awareness is also seen as the awareness that reflects from the Shri Amarnath Ji Yatra and Yatra Trail.

These cited Upanishadic verses of Figure 4 are from a theologically common understanding, are offerings, as Upanishadic Verses, of sacred realizations of our Vedic ancestors. Thus, this Yatra, is also a homage to our Vedic ancestors, as an act of realizing their offered realizations through the means of a Holy Yatra to Shri Amarnath Ji.

These verses, as depicted in this work, are a personal interpretation of the original texts, just as much as this rendering of this photo journal is a personal record of a personal Yatra to the Holy Cave of Shri Amarnath Ji.

As a human experience, each human experience is at best a human and a personal perspective.

Over the course of this photo journal, as reflective of the Holy Yatra and the Holy Yatra Trail, a particular and unique Upanishadic verse is rendered and realized through the means of a 'Yatra', that is a meditative realization, and also the 'Yatra Trail', the latter being a dualistic experience of a human journey of human physical observations, of human thoughts, and emotional experiences, and other human dimensions and perceptions, as the very human Yatri traverses the Holy Yatra Trail.

Thus, the non-dualistic realization, as self-evident in the cited Upanishadic verse, as an emanating Braham, is subsumed with the dualistic realization of the 'Oneness' by the Yatri, of all perceived human observations of the physical, the mental, the emotional, and other such perceptions.

This theme of the 'Yatra', the 'Yatra-trail', and the 'Yatri' as a subsumption process, a realization process, a 'presence' is realized, and re-affirmed or re-lived, as a celebration, as an emanation of the cited Upanishad Verses, over the realized experience of the Holy Shri Amarnath Ji Yatra. Thus, over the many cited unique Upanishadic Verses, a celebration of the Vedic realization of our Vedic Ancestors is realized. With reverence to our Vedic Ancestors, this homage is offered.

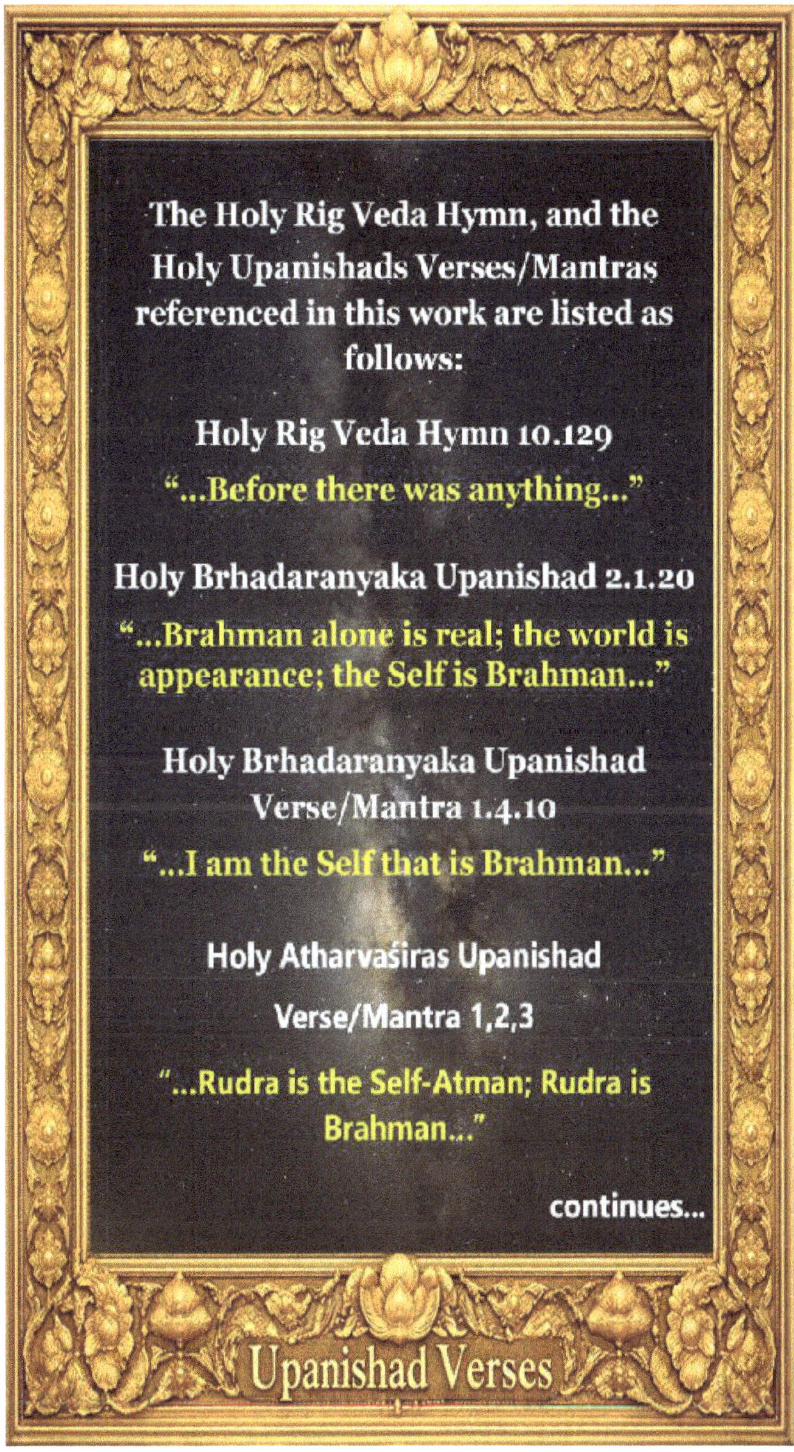
The Holy Rig Veda Hymn, and the Holy Upanishads Verses/Mantras referenced in this work are listed as follows:
Holy Rig Veda Hymn 10.129
"...Before there was anything..."
Holy Brhadaranyaka Upanishad 2.1.20
"...Brahman alone is real; the world is appearance; the Self is Brahman..."
Holy Brhadaranyaka Upanishad Verse/Mantra 1.4.10
"...I am the Self that is Brahman..."
Holy Atharvaśiras Upanishad
Verse/Mantra 1,2,3
"...Rudra is the Self-Atman; Rudra is Brahman..."
continues...
Upanishad Verses

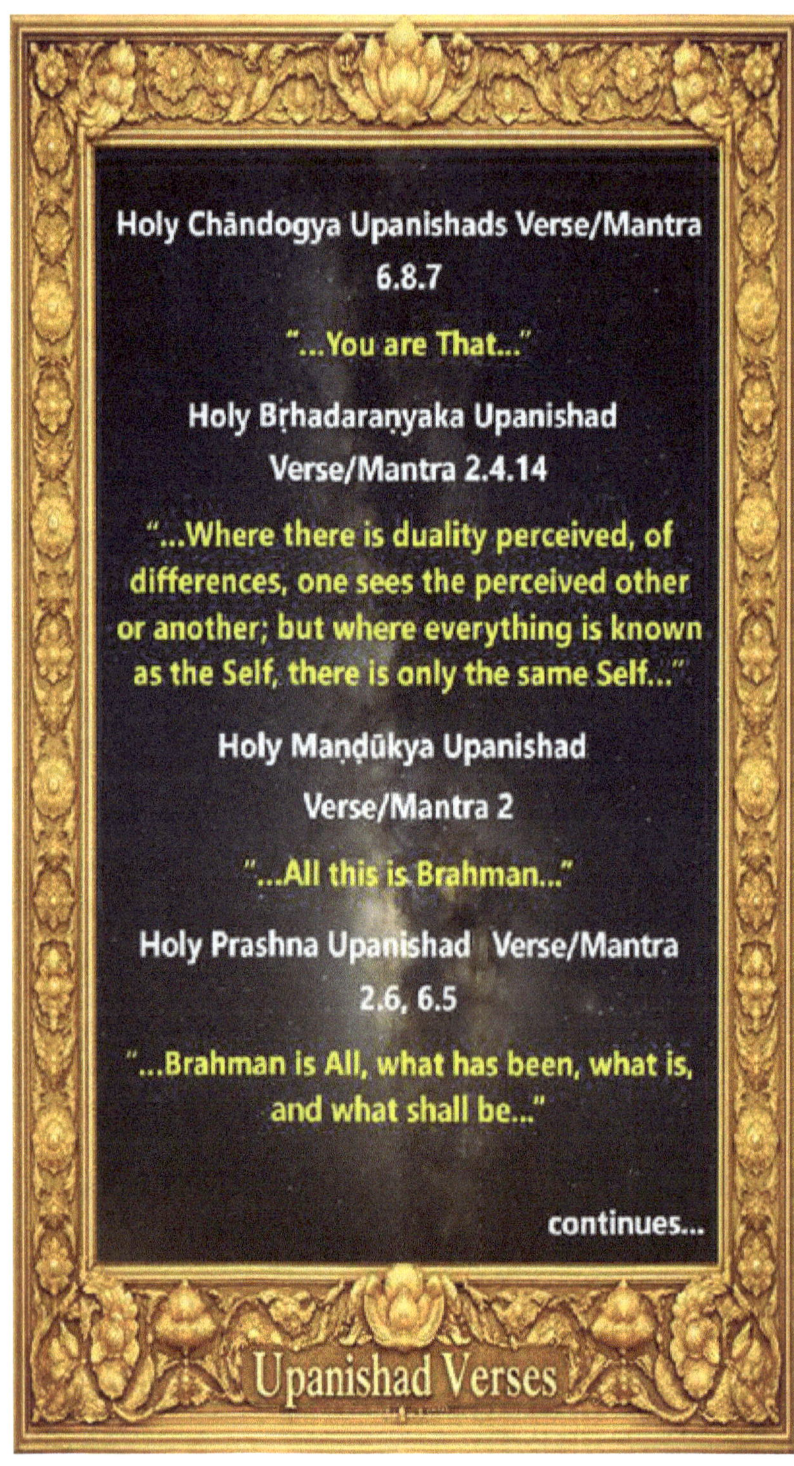
Holy Chāndogya Upanishads Verse/Mantra 6.8.7
"...You are That..."
Holy Bṛhadaraṇyaka Upanishad Verse/Mantra 2.4.14
"...Where there is duality perceived, of differences, one sees the perceived other or another; but where everything is known as the Self, there is only the same Self..."
Holy Maṇḍūkya Upanishad Verse/Mantra 2
"...All this is Brahman..."
Holy Prashna Upanishad Verse/Mantra 2.6, 6.5
"...Brahman is All, what has been, what is, and what shall be..."
continues...
Upanishad Verses

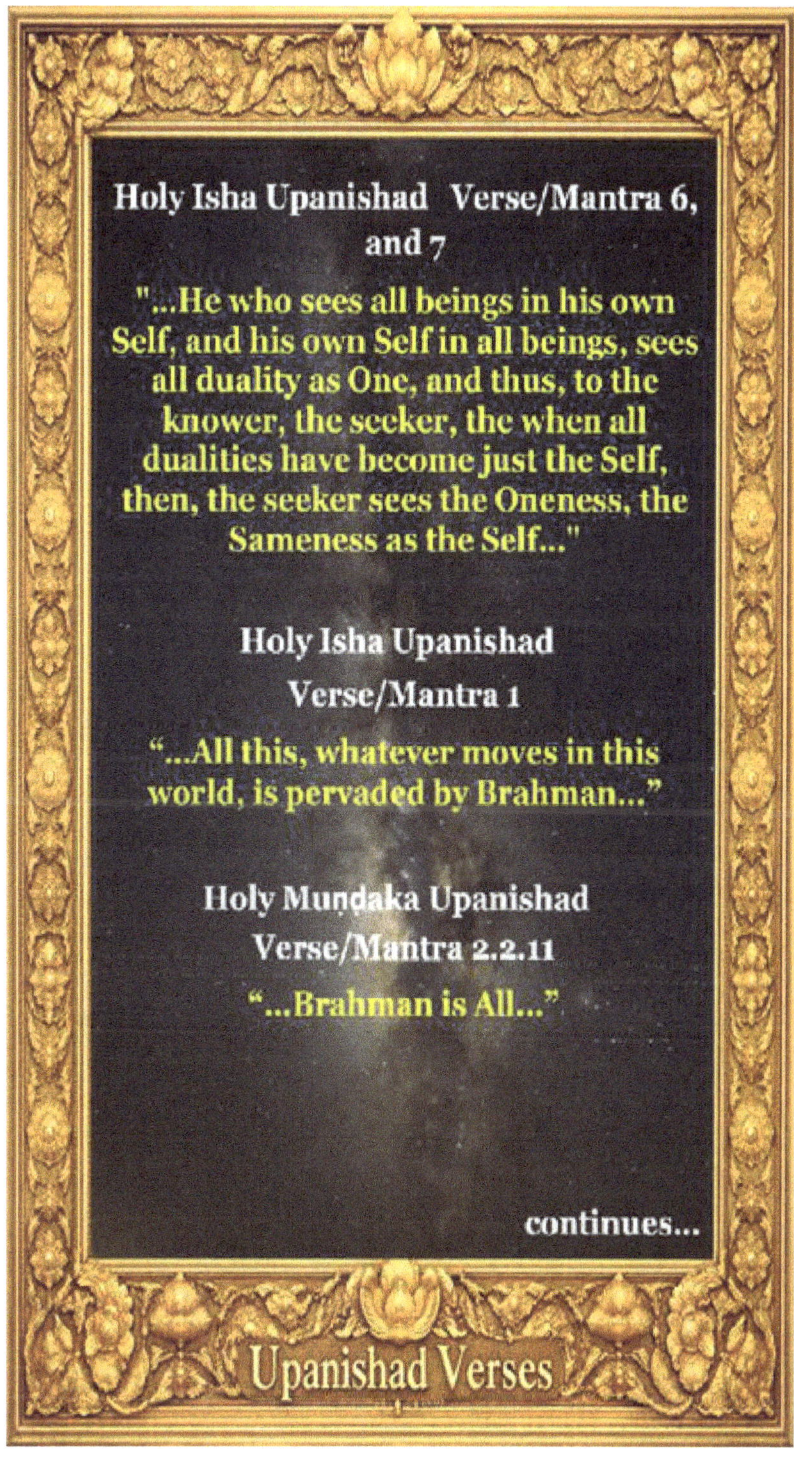
Holy Isha Upanishad Verse/Mantra 6, and 7
"...He who sees all beings in his own Self, and his own Self in all beings, sees all duality as One, and thus, to the knower, the seeker, the when all dualities have become just the Self, then, the seeker sees the Oneness, the Sameness as the Self..."
Holy Isha Upanishad
Verse/Mantra 1
"...All this, whatever moves in this world, is pervaded by Brahman..."
Holy Muṇḍaka Upanishad
Verse/Mantra 2.2.11
"...Brahman is All..."
continues...
Upanishad Verses

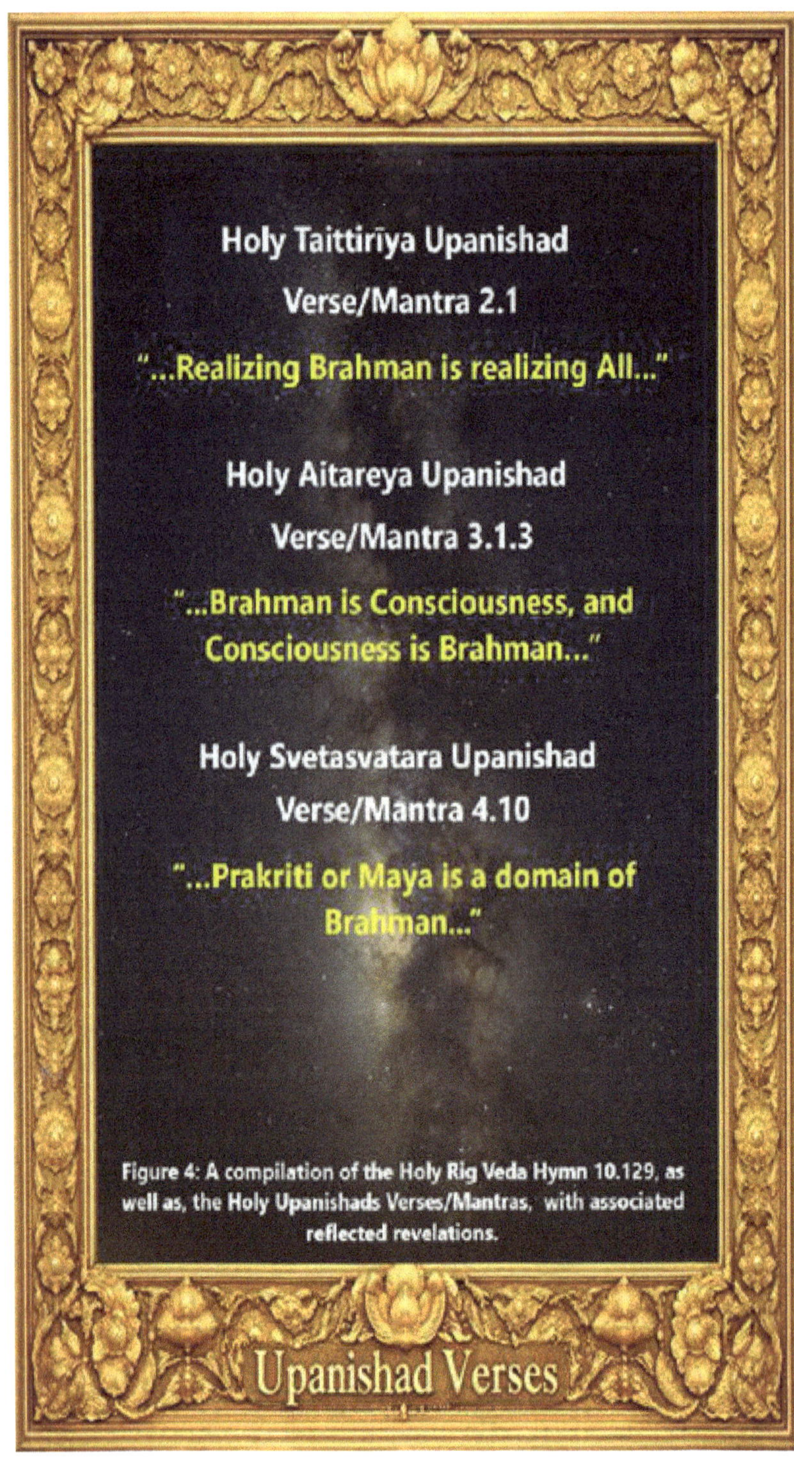


Figure 4: A compilation of the Holy Rig Veda Hymn 10.129, as well as, the Holy Upanishads Verses/Mantras, with associated reflected revelations.

## INTRODUCTION

This Yatra is a journal of an amalgam of several dimensions of a human experience and realizations that comprise:

- **A Spiritual Yatra**
- **A Physical Yatra**
- **A Mental Yatra**
- **An Emotional Yatra**

Common to all these dimensions is a deep reverence for the Holy Amarnath Ji Yatra and the Holy Yatra Trail. All human expressions expressed herein, are a simple an act of reverence, and also an act of devotion to the Holy Amarnath Ji Yatra and Yatra Trail.

A yatra is perhaps the most personal of human endeavors. Thus, the experiences described herein, the impressions described herein, are from the author's very human perspective, and are shared here in the spirit of reverence and devotion and celebration of Shri Amarnath Ji.

As such, this book attempts to present a mosaic of impressions of a yatra. This attempt, this portrayal of a reality, is akin to chasing a distant horizon, where your immediate perspective at a given point may be fixed, but with each progressive step, the horizon is continually redefined.

Thus, as you progress towards the horizon, and the horizon is continually rendered, a mosaic of continually resolving and refining impressions of the horizon take on new forms and perspectives.

Thus exists the world of human beings, the world of human reality. Within this human reality, there is a coexistent spirit of being. This spirit has, and maintains, an essential perspective. This essential perspective is timeless and unchanging. This essential perspective seeks no horizons. This essential perspective is absolute. This essential perspective sees only one thing. This essential perspective knows that it is on yatra. This essential perspective knows that this yatra is to the Abode of the Creator and Destroyer of all reality and all perspectives. This essential perspective, in prayer, in the deepest of devotion, with the deepest respect, is on its way to perform Darshan at the Holy Cave of Shri Amarnath Ji.

Thus, this account, this rendering of a yatra, is a personal perspective of the horizon, detailed as a particular set of experiences, reflections, and impressions.

A note about the places and names used in this book:

Several slightly variant spellings exist in the literature, and common usage, for some of the places on the Yatra Trail.

Specifically, a reference in this work to “Pisu Hill” or “Pisu Hill Top” is also a reference to “Phishutop”, or Pissu hill”, “Pisu Top”, or the like common or local usage. Similarly, a reference to “Chandanwari”, is also a reference to “Chandanwadi”, or the like common or local usage. Also, a reference to “Panchtarni” is also a reference to “Panjtarni”, or the like common usage. Also, similar variants in nomenclature exist for other local places, however, all such places are situated in this book with appropriate context.

A note on the scope of this book:

There are five parts (Part 1, through Part 5, inclusive) or elements to this book. These parts are inter-related and threaded in the following sequence.

**Part one:** The introduction provides an orientation to the subject matter.

**Part two:** Next, by the medium of a journal, a first-hand impression of the journey, which for the author is a yatra, is detailed.

**Part three:** A personal Darshan is realized.

**Part four:** Next, offered are some personal impressions of the Yatra. Here a discourse, a meditation on a personal journey is shared.

**Part five:** Finally, for the would-be traveler, some notes are provided for the preparation of a trek.

Also, interleaved within the body of this book, are citations of Sacred Verses, or Sacred Mantras, from the Sacred Upanishads.

These cited Sacred Upanishads, and the Sacred Verses/Mantras are available in the present-day public domain literature.

The selected Sacred Verses/Mantras from the selected Sacred Upanishads, that resonates with the realization of Advaita Brahman, are presented herein, in the body of this book, as an act of reverence, an act of devotion, an act of a meditative process, as the cited Verses/Mantras, to the author, to the seeker, in a personal and human realization, resonate with the spirit of the Yatra, and the Yatra Trail, of the Shri Amarnath Ji Yatra.

# PART ONE:

# AN ORIENTATION TO SHRI AMARNATH JI:

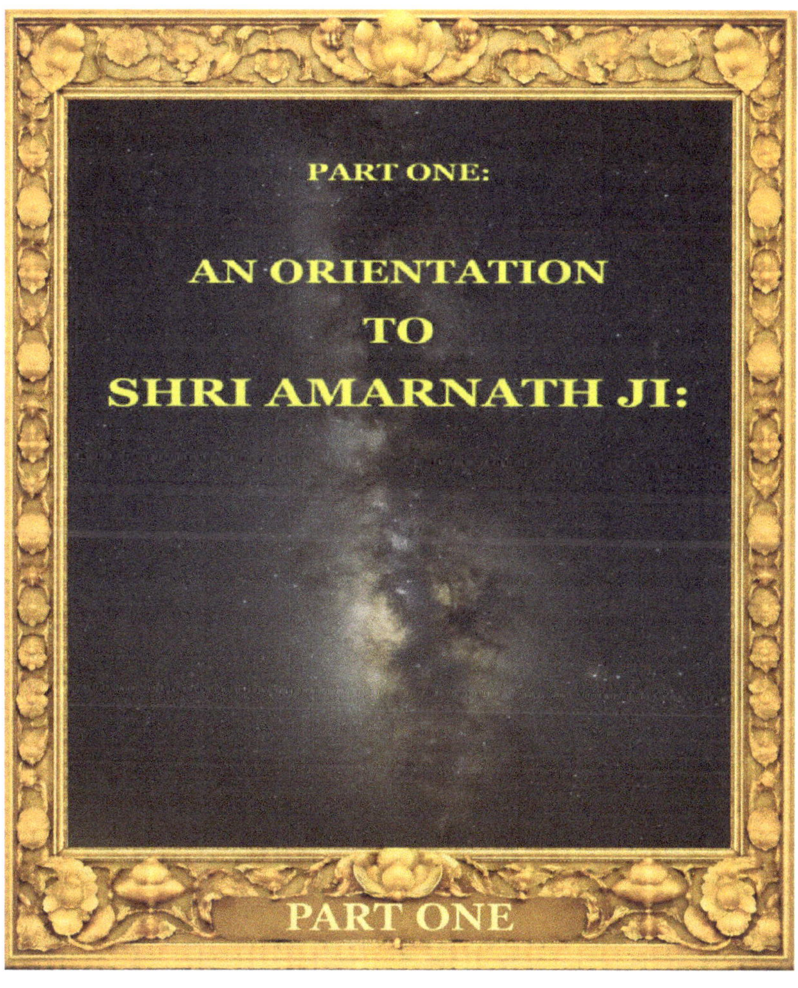

## A PERSPECTIVEOF SHRI AMARNATH JI

In the Indian Western Himalayas, in the region known as Kashmir, there exists at an altitude of 7500 ft, a small alpine town named Pahalgam. Pahalgam serves as a gateway to the Himalayan Mountain ranges that loom above and about its periphery. Among the many Himalayan corridors that open from Pahalgam, there is a path, a trail, a Holy Trail, that leads you to the Himalayan Holy cave of Shri Amarnath Ji. The Holy Cave of Shri Amarnath Ji is the abode of Lord Shiva, the creator and the destroyer of the universe.

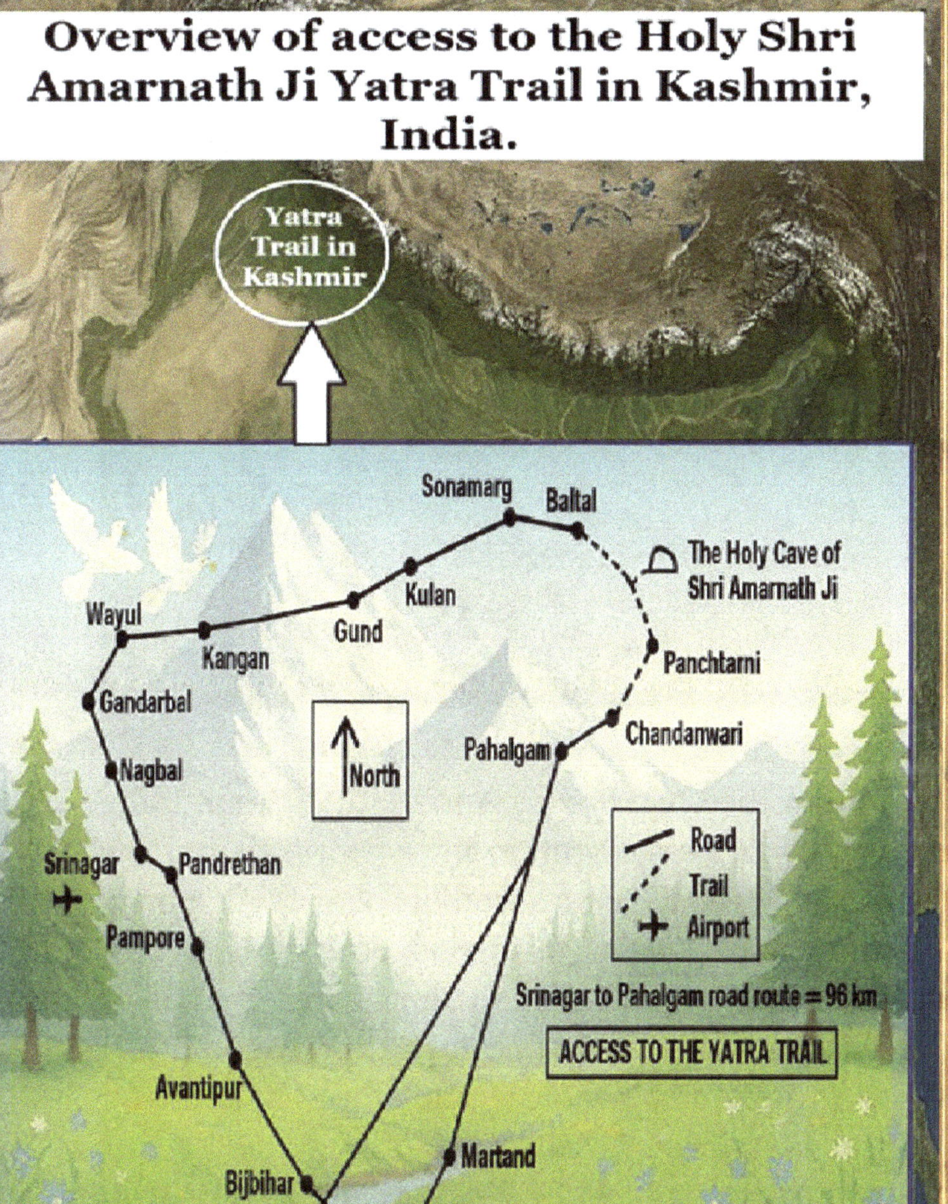


# OVERVIEW MAP

A view from the air...the Kashmir mountains were calling...The Shri Amarnath Ji Yatra Trail was calling...without hesitation...I followed my calling...

Within the Cave of Shri Amarnath Ji, a naturally occurring ice-stalagmite, in the form of an Ice lingam, which is a symbol of Lord Shiva, miraculously takes form year after year. yatris, devotees, year after year, during the month of Shravan (July- August), come to Shri Amarnath Ji to witness and behold Templethis Miracle, and seek Blessings from their Maker.

It is said that, during the Full Moon of Shravan, which is also called Shravan-Purnima, the Holy Ice-Lingum reaches it's greatest height. The Ice-Lingum is said to wax and wane with the Moon. It is also said that by the side of the Holy Ice-Lingum associated with Lord Shiva, two more Ice-lingums also form, and are associated with Parvati Ji, the Wife of Lord Shiva, and Ganesh Ji, the Son of Shiv-Parvati Ji.

## A SHARED LEGEND

A summary of a commonly shared '**Legend**' associated with the Holy Cave of Shri Amarnath Ji is respectfully shared below.

As a preamble to the beginning of the holy yatra to Shri Amarnat Ji, a Darshan at the Shri Shankaracharya Ji Temple in Kasmir became a natural step.

A Darshan at Shri Shankaracharya Ji Temple in Srinagar Kashmir

Immediately, having performed Darshan at Shri Shankaracharya Ji Temple, an inner bliss started to be invoked that resonated with "...I am the Self that is Brahman...".

Thus, a Self-realization process of Seeking Brahman, Knowing Brahman, and Being Brahman, as reflected in the Holy Rig Vedas and the Holy Upanishads, while walking on the Holy Yatra Trail became the solitary path for the trekker, the hiker, the walker, that had by such realizations had transformed into a Yatri.

This realization of the Self the revelation of our Vedic Ancestors in the form of the Holy Rig Veda and the Upanishads became the guide for the Yatri on the Holy Yatra Trail of Shri Amarnath Ji.

An element of this Vedic guidance is the Holy Brhadaranyaka Upanishad Verse 1.4.10., which emanates the Vedic realization that "...I am the Self that is Brahman...".

The Holy Brhadaranyaka Upanishad Verse 1.4.10., is depicted below and along with it is the Yatri's very human meditations of this Vedic realization as it related to the Yatri on the Holy Yatra Trail of Shri Amarnath Ji.

Similarly, throughout the balance of this journal of the Yatra to the Holy Cave of Shri Amarnath Ji, other Vedic Upanishads that resonates with the realizations Shri Shankaracharya Ji, and particularly, resonates with the realization of Brahman, are with reverence realized here.

In this theme of the Yatri's meditations on the revelations of our Vedic Ancestors, the Yatra is manifested.

## Holy Brhadaranyaka Upanishad, Verse 1.4.10: Revelation

Herein, Verse 1.4.10 of the Holy Brhadaranyaka Upanishad became the object of meditation—both the realization and the lived reality of the Yatri on the Yatra Trail.

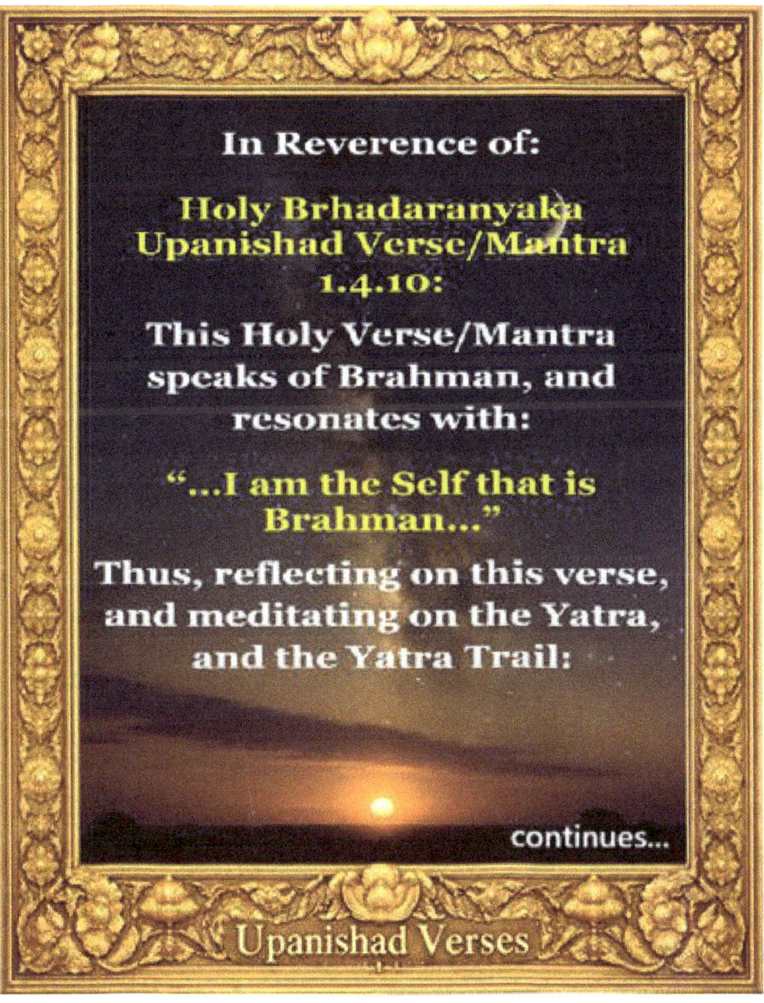

## Holy Brhadaranyaka Upanishad, Verse 1.4.10: Realizations on the Yatra Trail

## Holy Brhadaranyaka Upanishad, Verse 1.4.10: Realizations on the Yatra Trail

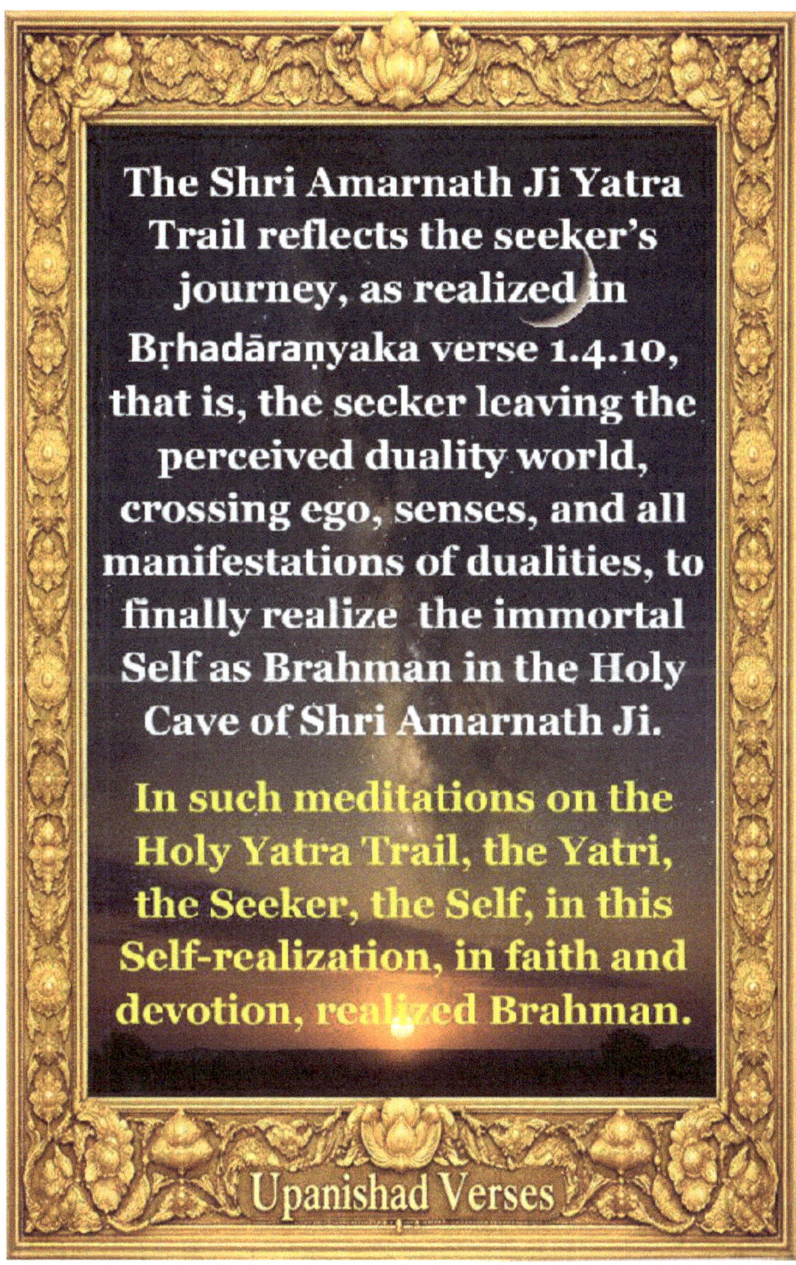

# A PERSPECTIVE OF SHRI AMARNATH JI YATRA AND YATRA TRAIL:

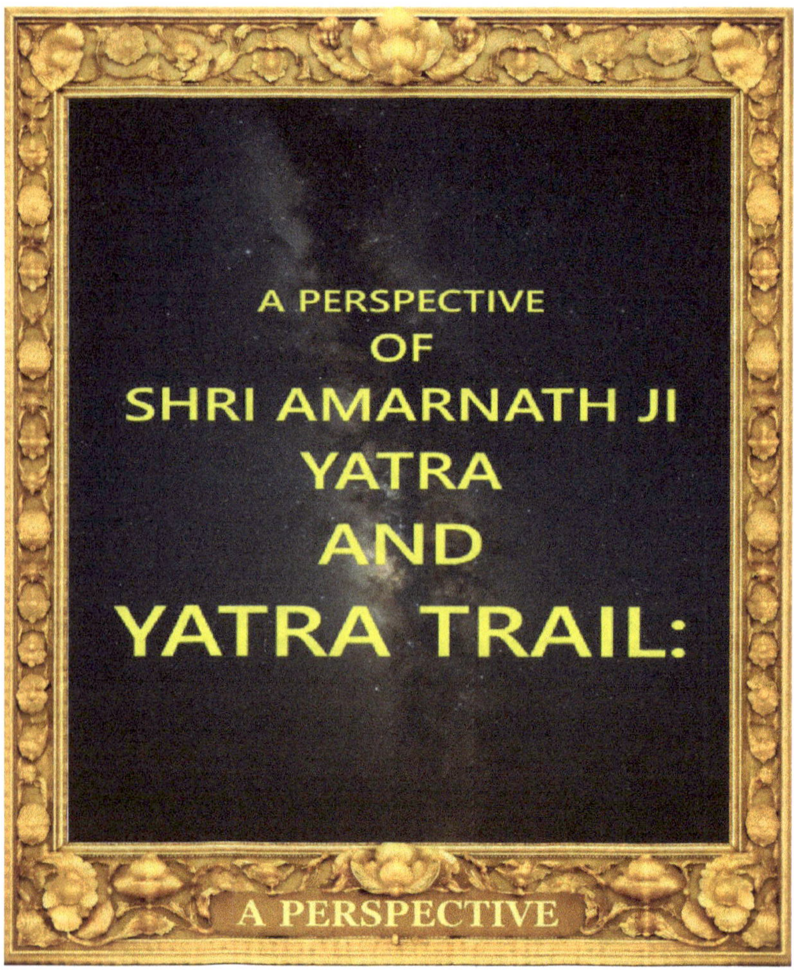

Although the traditional yatra commences from Srinagar, the following discussion describes the Yatra undertaken from Pahalgam to the Holy Cave of Shri Amarnath Ji. The alpine town of Pahalgam has become an assembly point for the embarkation of the traditional Himalayan segment of the yatra.

The Physical journey from Pahalgam to the holy cave of Shri Amarnath Ji progresses through a spectacular Himalayan corridor. This journey takes you through an alpine countryside, along glacial streams, around a glacial lake, over a mountain pass, over snow bridges, and finally terminating at the sacred mountain cave of Shri Amarnath Ji. This yatra, this journey, is not just a physical journey; this yatra, this journey, is a yatra of the body, mind, and the spirit.

A Billboard of the Route Map of Shri Amarnath Ji Track in Pahalgam.

The one-way distance from Pahalgam to the Holy cave is 30 miles. In this writing, this 30 mile trek is highlighted as a series of 6 trail segments. A summary of these yatra trail segments is highlighted as follows.

- **Pahalgam to Chandanwari.**

From the alpine town of Pahalgam, at 7500 ft., to Chandanwari, at a distance of 10 miles and at a height of 9500 ft.

- **Chandanwari to Pisu Hill Top.**

From Chandanwari to the top of Pisu Hill, with steeply ascending switchbacks near the top of the hill. Pisu Hill at a distance of 2 miles, and at an altitude of 11500 ft.

- **Pisu Hill Top to Sheshnag Lake.**

Next, the yatra trail from Pisu Hill, over a distance of 6 miles, along Sheshnag stream, would reach Sheshnag Lake, at an altitude of 12200 ft.

- **Sheshnag Lake to Mahagunas Pass.**

From Sheshnag Lake, the 3 mile ascent to Mahagunas Pass (14800 ft.). This segment reaches the highest point on the Trail.

- **Mahagunas Pass to Panchtarni**.

From Mahagunas Pass, a gradual descent over 5 miles, to reach Panchtarni at an altitude of 11500 ft.

- **Panchtarni to the Holy Cave of Shri Amarnath Ji.**

Finally, a 4-mile trek to the Holy Cave of Shri Amarnath Ji, at an altitude of 13500 ft.

## Holy Atharvaśiras Upanishad, Verses 1,2,3: Revelation

Herein, Verses 1, 2, and 3 of the Holy Atharvaśiras Upanishad became the object of meditation—at once the realization and the lived reality of the Yatri on the Yatra Trail.

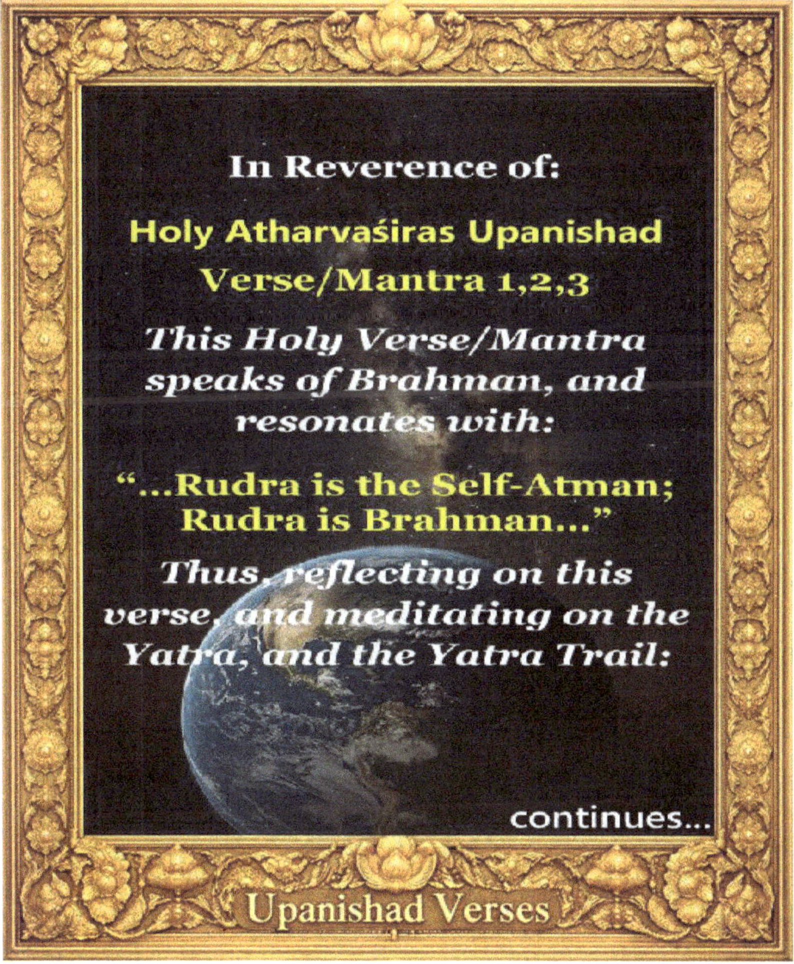

## Holy Atharvaśiras Upanishad, Verses 1,2,3: Realizations on the Yatra Trail

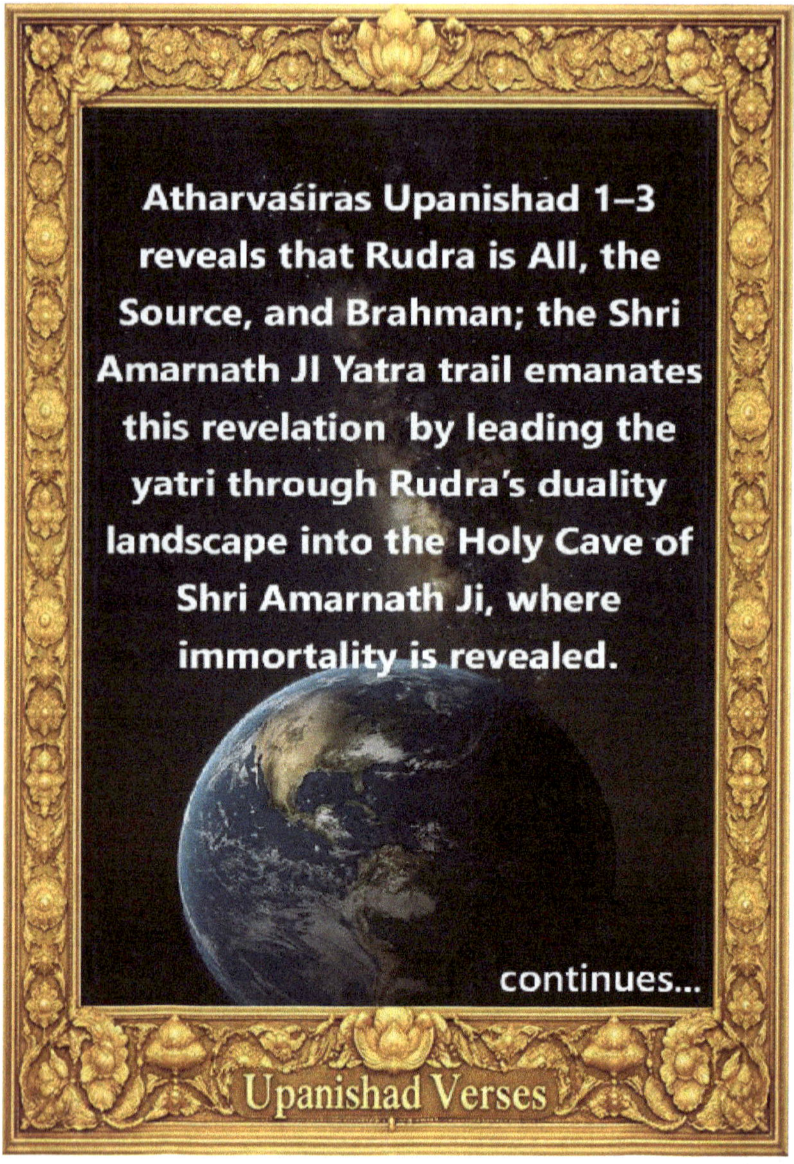

# Holy Atharvaśiras Upanishad, Verses 1,2,3: Realizations on the Yatra Trail

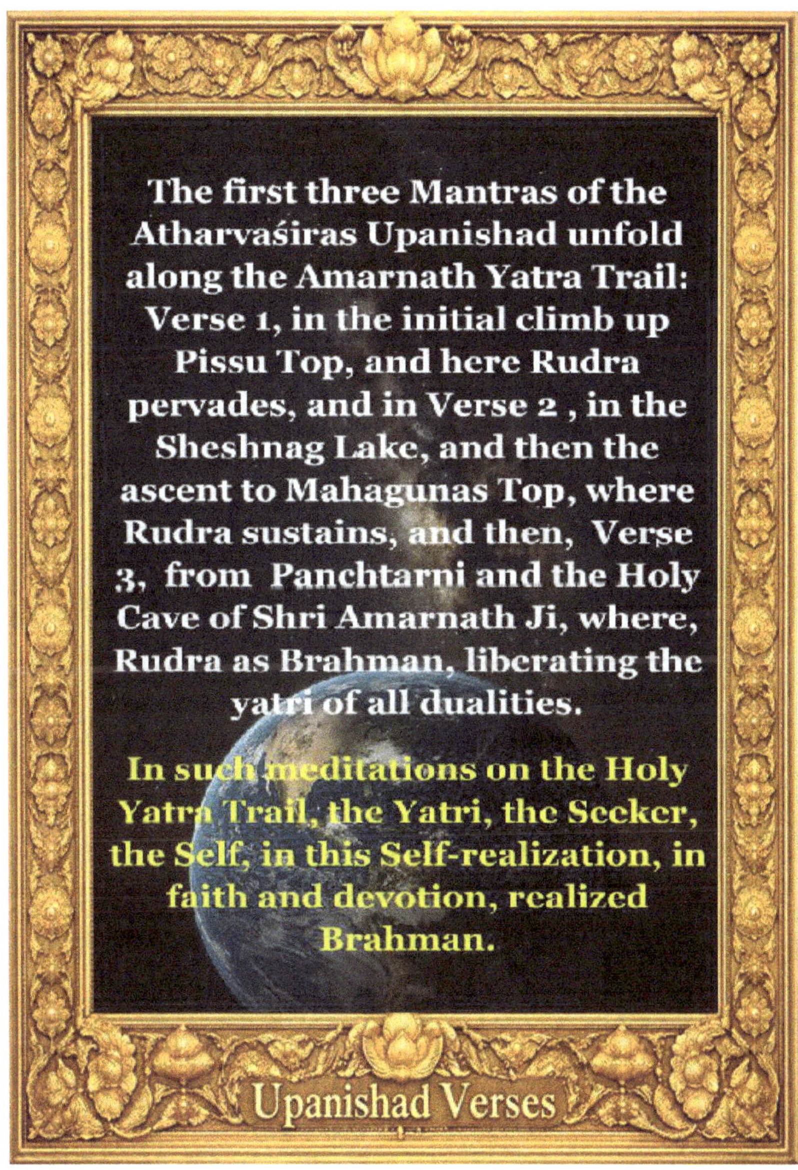

# PART TWO:

# SHRI AMARNATH JI YATRA TRAIL YATRA:

**The following Six sections of this book describe the complete Shri Amarnath Ji Yatra Trail and Yatra.**

The Yatra Trail starts from the town of Pahalgam and finishes at the Holy Cave of Shri Amarnath JI.

The six sections of the Shri Amarnath Yatra Trail, that comprise the six physical segments of the Shri Amarnath Ji Trail, are summarized as follows:

**Section 1:** Pahalgam to Chandanwari segment

**Section 2:** Chandanwari to Pisu Hill Top segment

**Section 3:** Pisu Hill Top to Sheshnag Lake segment

**Section 4:** Sheshnag Lake to Mahagunas Pass segment

**Section 5:** Mahagunas Pass to Panchtarni segment

**Section 6:** Panchtarni to the Holy Cave of Shri Amarnath Ji segment

The six sections that follow this Yatra Trail summary are the detailed descriptions that seek to embody the Shri Amarnath Ji Yatra Trail and Yatra to the Holy Cave of Shri Amarnath Ji personal experience.

The following figure, titled 'YATRA TRAIL'S ALTITUDE PROFILE', depicts the entire Shri Amarnath JI Yatra Trail as experienced and detailed within the scope of this book. The noted figure, titled 'YATRA TRAIL'S ALTITUDE PROFILE', also provides for the stages of the Shri Amarnath Ji Yatra Trail, starting from the basecamp town of Pahalgam, and culminating at the destination of the Holy Cave of Shri Amarnath Ji. The noted figure also depecits the prominent stages of the Yatra trail traversed during the Holy Yatra, wherein, the stages are detailed within the noted figure with the stage's name, altitude of the stage, as well as the distance, in miles, from the basecamp of Pahalgam, as traversed over the Yatra Trail.

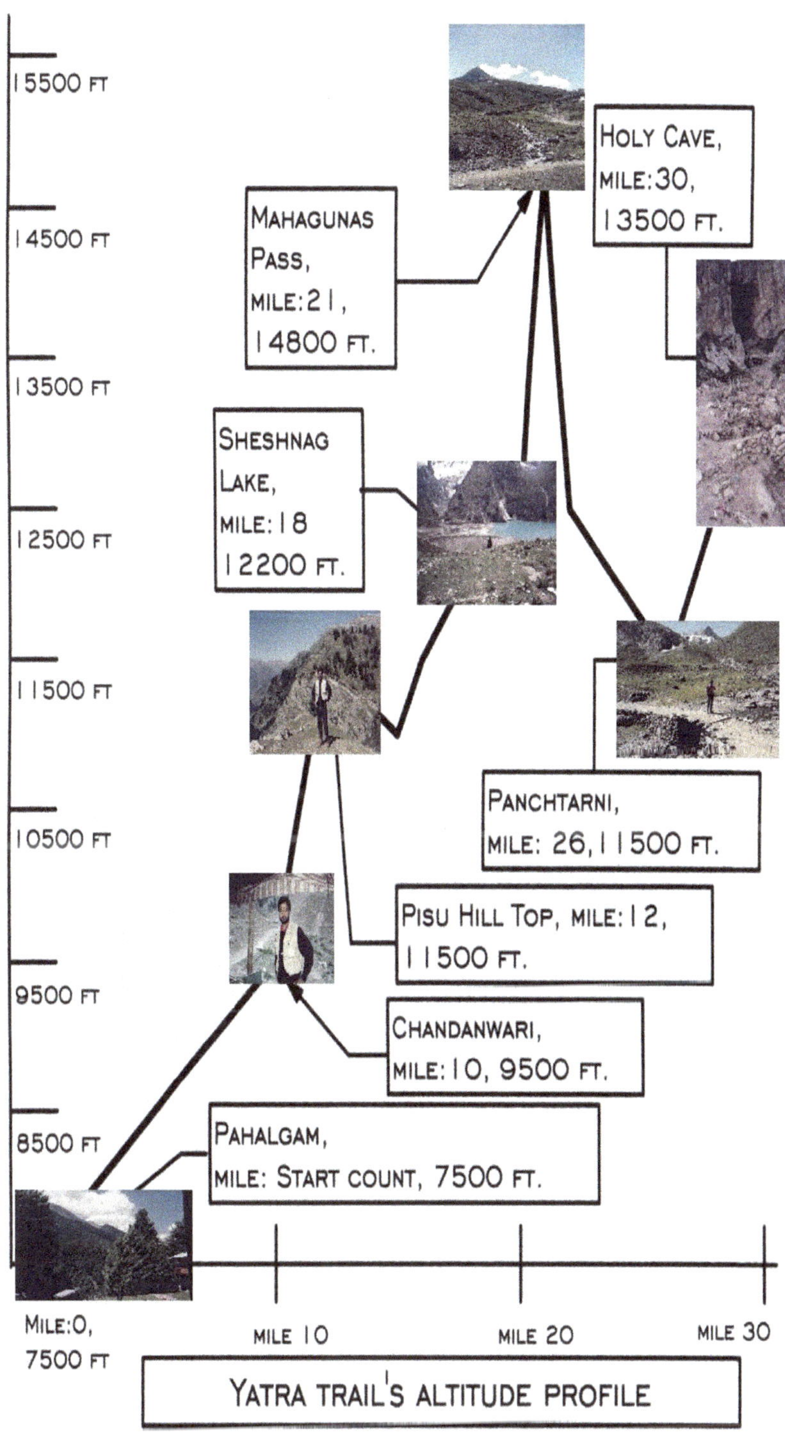
15500 FT
14500 FT
13500 FT
12500 FT
11500 FT
10500 FT
9500 FT
8500 FT
MAHAGUNAS PASS, MILE:21, 14800 FT.
HOLY CAVE, MILE:30, 13500 FT.
SHESHNAG LAKE, MILE:18 12200 FT.
PANCHTARNI, MILE: 26, 11500 FT.
PISU HILL TOP, MILE:12, 11500 FT.
CHANDANWARI, MILE:10, 9500 FT.
PAHALGAM, MILE: START COUNT, 7500 FT.
MILE:0, 7500 FT
MILE 10
MILE 20
MILE 30
YATRA TRAIL'S ALTITUDE PROFILE

## Holy Chāndogya Upanishad, Verse 6.8.7: Revelation

Herein, Verse 6.8.7 of the Holy Chāndogya Upanishad became the object of meditation—at once the realization and the lived reality of the Yatri on the Yatra Trail.

## Holy Chāndogya Upanishad, Verse 6.8.7: Realizations on the Yatra Trail

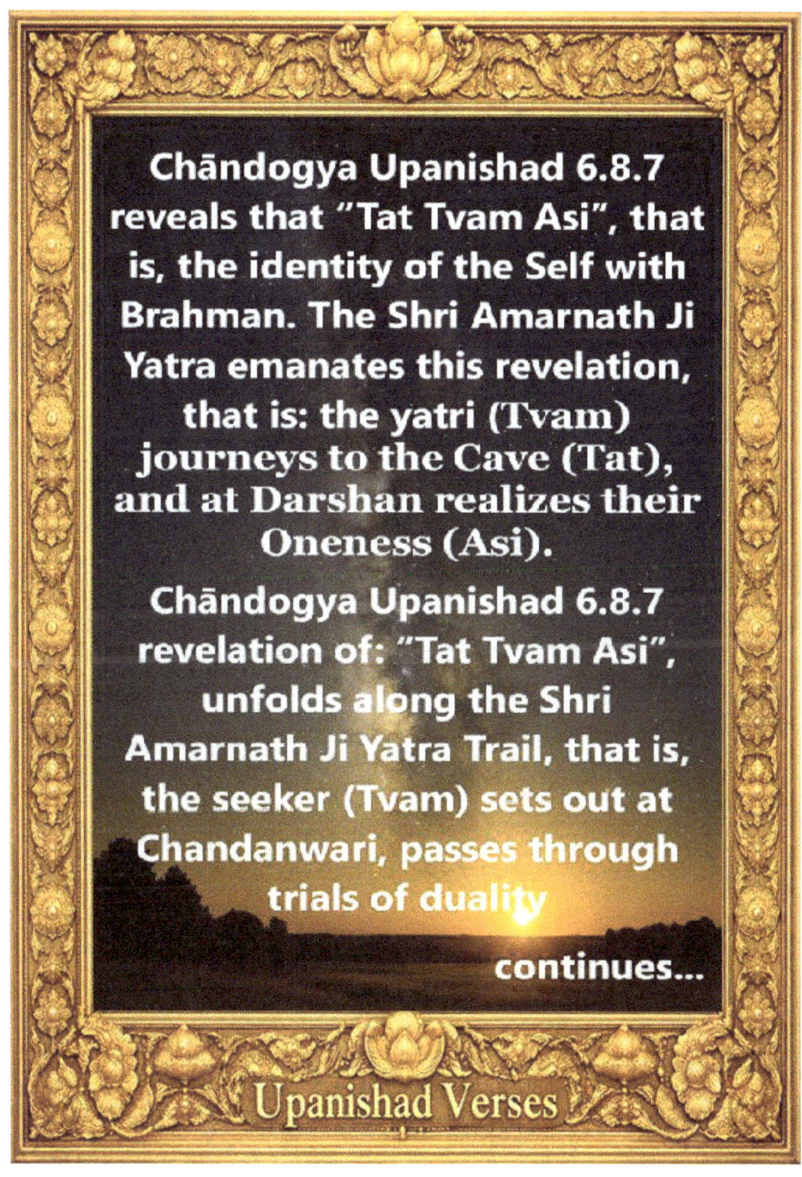

## Holy Chāndogya Upanishad, Verse 6.8.7: Realizations on the Yatra Trail

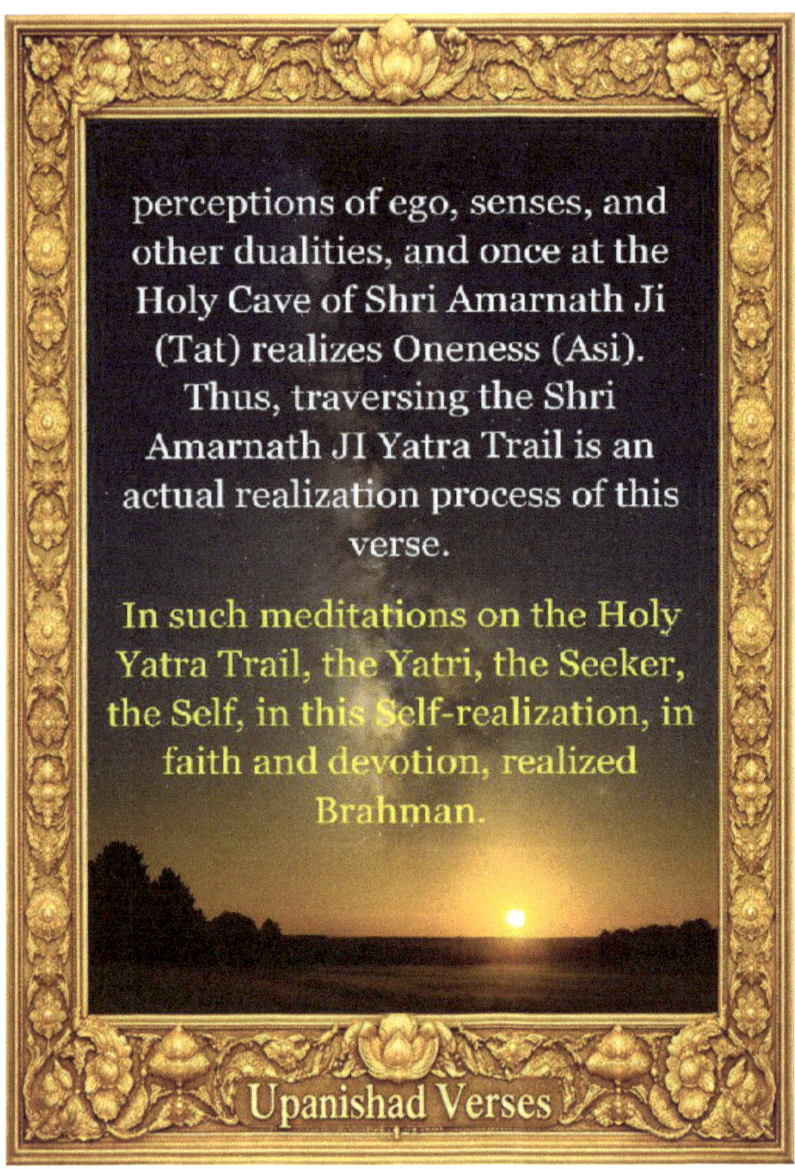

# YATRA TRAIL SECTION 1:

# PAHALGAM TO CHANDANWARI YATRA:

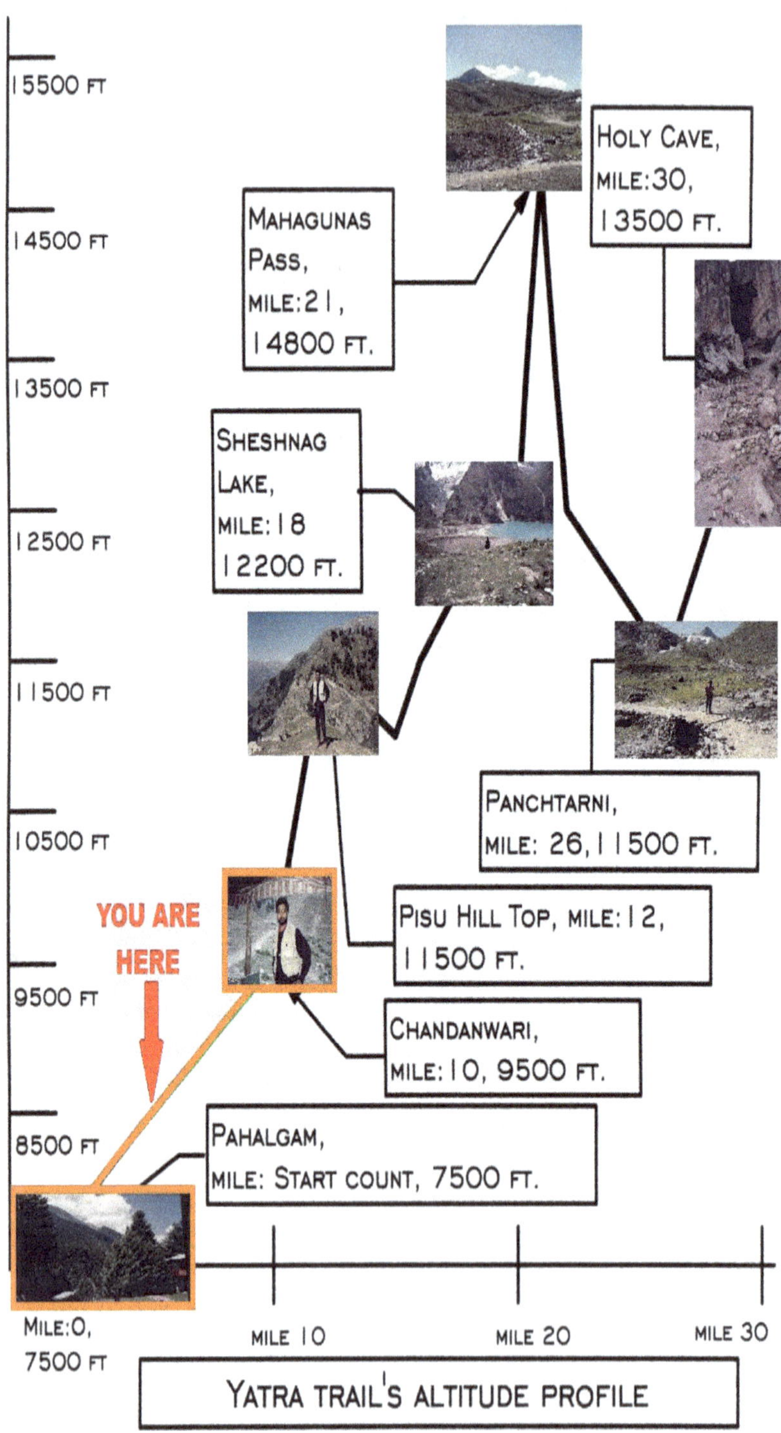
15500 FT
14500 FT
13500 FT
12500 FT
11500 FT
10500 FT
9500 FT
8500 FT
HOLY CAVE, MILE:30, 13500 FT.
MAHAGUNAS PASS, MILE:21, 14800 FT.
SHESHNAG LAKE, MILE:18 12200 FT.
PANCHTARNI, MILE: 26, 11500 FT.
PISU HILL TOP, MILE:12, 11500 FT.
YOU ARE HERE
CHANDANWARI, MILE:10, 9500 FT.
PAHALGAM, MILE: START COUNT, 7500 FT.
MILE:0, 7500 FT
MILE 10
MILE 20
MILE 30
YATRA TRAIL'S ALTITUDE PROFILE

## Terrain Characteristics:

### Pahalgam to Chandanwari:

**Environment:** Sub-alpine forested valley.

**Area features**: lush pine forests, meadows, rivers and water stream.

**This was it. You were there. You were in Pahalgam for your yatra to Shri Amarnath Ji.**

Pahalgam was a small and a quiet little alpine town. In Pahalgam, people and shops and the occasional traffic of automobiles was a part of a well-orchestrated movement of daily activity. Pahalgam was reflective of all that a picturesque alpine town could be.

There were camping stores, photography stores, restaurants, hotels, . . ., yes, it was all here. Pahalgam was alive with purpose and meaning and colors and sounds that kept you mesmerized. You found yourself easily becoming a part of Pahalgam. However, you had come to Pahalgam with a purpose.

Your purpose, your inner voice, had commanded you to be here. Now, the same calling was compelling you to detach yourself from the harmony of activity of Pahalgam and caused you to gaze at the horizon. There at the horizon, around the periphery of the town of Pahalgam were towering Himalayan peaks standing in silence. Beyond these silent towering peaks was the Holy Cave of Shri Amarnath Ji. The silence of the mountains beyond was calling you.

A Pahalgam lodge with a view of the beckoning mountains in the background that were your calling...

Reflectively, you kept looking at the silent peaks again and again. You knew you had to go towards them. There was no doubt in your knowing. You just smiled a knowing smile. With a single focus, you looked at the silent peaks and prayed silently.

The morning of your yatra from Pahalgam to Shri Amarnath Ji arrived. You awakened to a day when your intent was to become an actuality. Thus, on that morning, in a blissful exuberance, you headed for the Shri Amarnath Ji yatra trail.

From Pahalgam, the yatra trail started essentially at the edge of Pahalgam's main street, where several billboards provided you with a general bearing of Pahalgam and it's environment. One large billboard displayed a trail map of the entire length of the Shri Amarnath Ji yatra trail. This trail map, a detailed perspective summary of the

Alpine slopes lined the gateway of Pahalgam to Chandanwari journey

yatra trail, included the yatra trail's major physical features, milestones, distances between milestones, altitudes of selected points, and facilities such as shelters present along the yatra trail. Another billboard, with a large red painted arrow, pointed towards Chandanwari. Chandanwari was the first milestone on your way to Shri Amarnath Ji. A step in the direction of Chandanwari was a step onto the holy yatra trail.

Thus, with the deepest devotion, you stepped in the direction of Chandanwari and as such onto the yatra trail. In this simple and meaningful act, you left Pahalgam behind and were on your way to the Holy Cave of Shri Amarnath Ji.

The yatra trail from Pahalgam steepened and maneuvered through the adjoining alpine mountainside. Your ascending journey continued. The air was cool, mountain fresh, and clear. The sunlight was crisp and warm and comforting. You were in a fixed state of exuberance. In just a matter of a few hours you were in a different reality, a reality of a solitary trail high in the mountains, headed towards Chandanwari. Below, you could look at the pastoral land adjoining Pahalgam encircled by alpine trees. The world that was now left behind, started to fade into a distant reality. You were now one with the very same mountains that you adored and worshiped from Pahalgam.

The slow physical progression from Pahalgam to Chandanwari could not compete with the racing mind. Thoughts of people, places, and things, thoughts of why, what and where, idle thoughts, endless thoughts, were being mixed with the visual panorama of an alpine mountainside that was unfolding before you. As you persisted higher and higher on the mountain trail, the physical world was changing, also, that which you called your very self was changing.

In this process of change, or more so a clarifying process, a refocus and a perspective of the larger scheme of things started to dawn on you. A simplicity started to assert itself. This was not just a physical journey, it became an inescapable

A view from Chandanwari Yatra Trail Head, with the Shri Amarnath Ji Yatra Trail in the background

realization that this was a journey of the very self, the very being.

You started to notice the many small and yet meaningful details of Pahalgam, and of your life as well, becoming a part of a larger view and meaning of life. A recursive re-definition of the self-started to emerge. A detachment from the familiarities and the complexities of your world started to yield to a kind of an attachment to a simpler reality. A simple reason or cause had put you on this yatra trail. That simplicity was the answer to it all. You embraced that simplicity, that truth, and prayed and smiled. The mind kept fading between a sensory bliss and a solitude of the newly discovered self. In this awareness you kept moving, on your way to Chandanwari.

Soon, without much of a pronouncement, you reached your first milestone, the small and quiet little outpost called Chandanwari. Here at Chandanwari, the air started to feel a bit crisper and an indication of the rarified air ahead on the yatra trail became obvious.

From Pahalgam, at a height of 7500 ft, there was a gradual increase of the trails altitude, and after a net altitude gain of 2000 ft, over a distance of ten miles, you arrived at Chandanwari, at a height of 9500 ft.

**A view from the Shri Amarnath Ji Yatra Trail Head in Chandanwari, with the ascending Yatra Trail in the background**

A view from
Pahalgam of the
Alpine surroundings.

## Holy Bṛhadāraṇyaka Upanishad, Verse 2.4.14: Revelation

Herein, Verse 2.4.14 of the Holy Bṛhadāraṇyaka Upanishad became the object of meditation—both the realization and the lived reality of the Yatri upon the Yatra Trail.

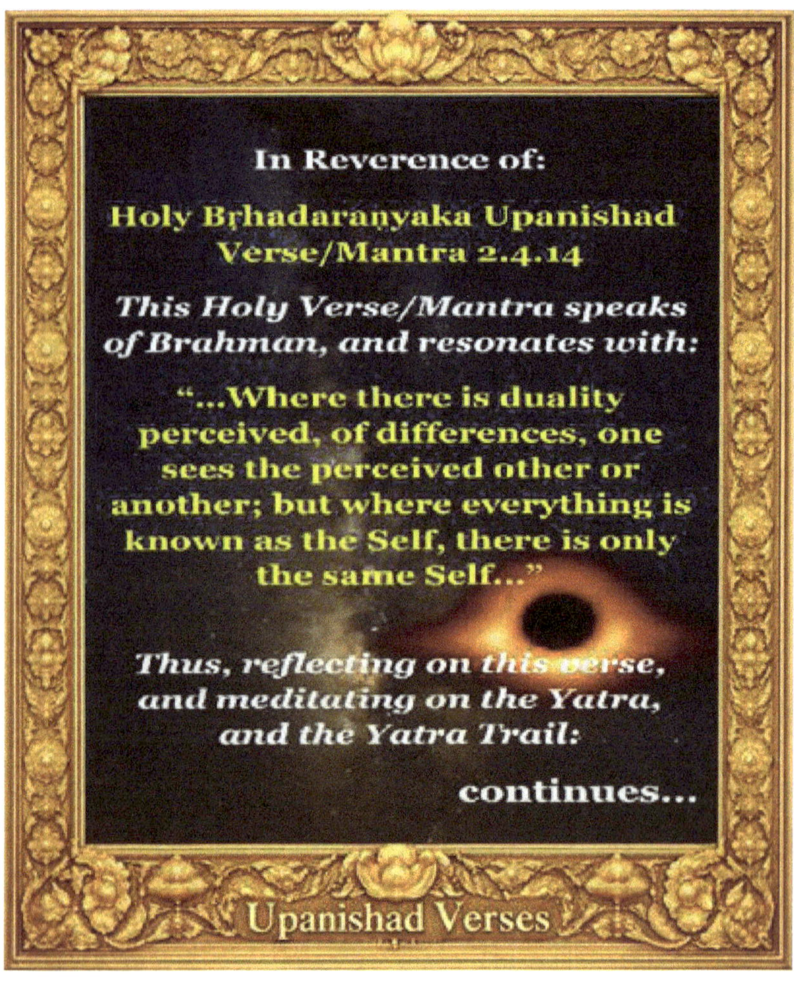

## Holy Bṛhadāraṇyaka Upanishad, Verse 2.4.14: Realizations on the Yatra Trail

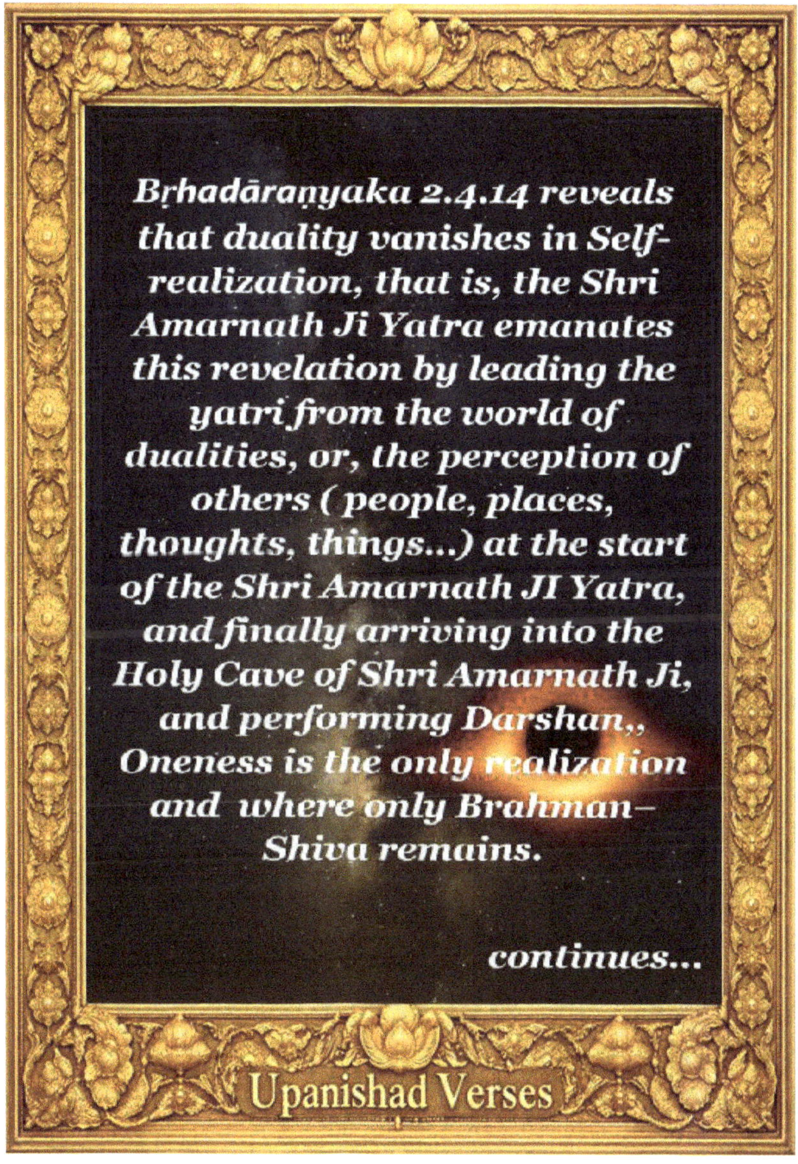

## Holy Bṛhadāraṇyaka Upanishad, Verse 2.4.14: Realizations on the Yatra Trail

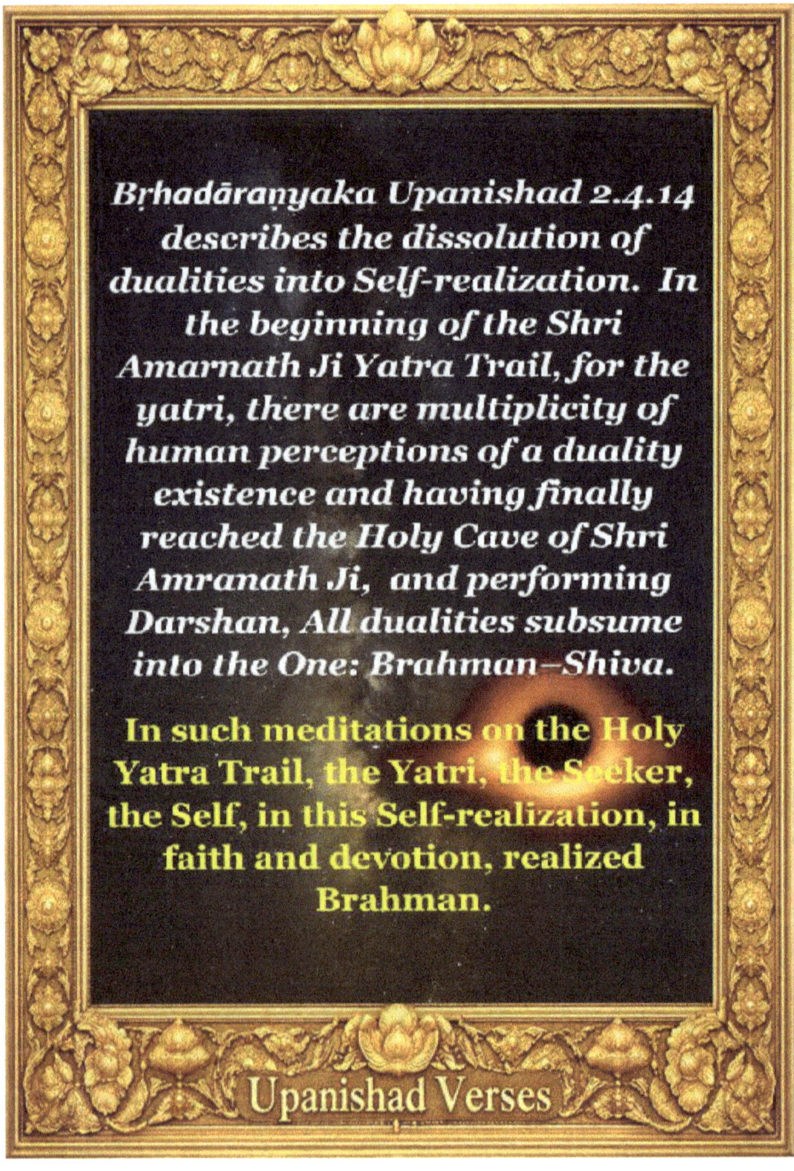

# YATRA TRAIL SECTION 2:

# CHANDANWARI TO PISU TOP YATRA:

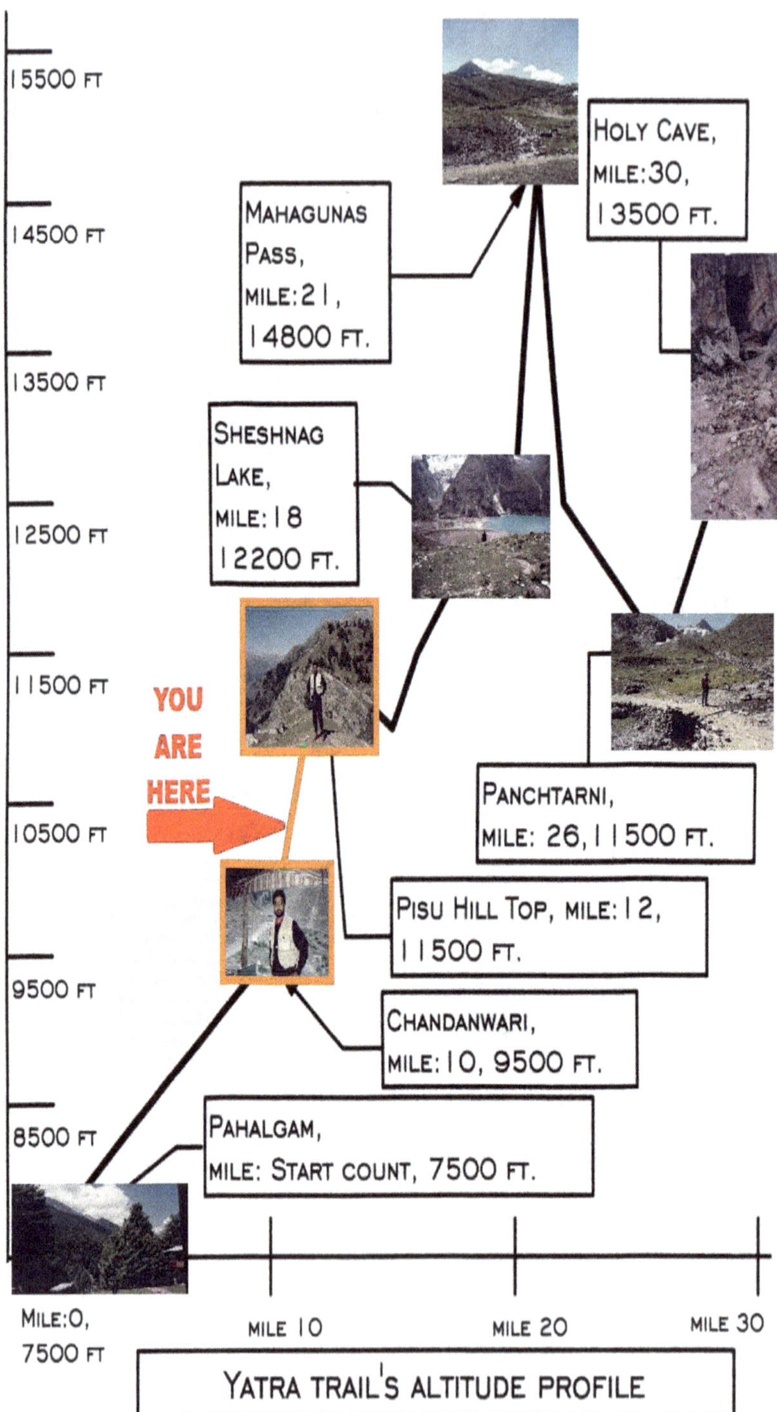
15500 FT
14500 FT
13500 FT
12500 FT
11500 FT
10500 FT
9500 FT
8500 FT
HOLY CAVE,
MILE:30,
13500 FT.
MAHAGUNAS
PASS,
MILE:21,
14800 FT.
SHESHNAG
LAKE,
MILE:18
12200 FT.
YOU
ARE
HERE
PANCHTARNI,
MILE: 26, 11500 FT.
PISU HILL TOP, MILE: 12,
11500 FT.
CHANDANWARI,
MILE: 10, 9500 FT.
PAHALGAM,
MILE: START COUNT, 7500 FT.
MILE:0,
7500 FT
MILE 10
MILE 20
MILE 30
YATRA TRAIL'S ALTITUDE PROFILE

## Terrain Characteristics:

### Chandanwari to Pissu Top:

**Environment:** Alpine zone: tree lines begin to thin; steep rocky climbs; meadows interspersed

**Area features:** feels like early alpine ascent: with grassy slopes giving way to rock and sparse vegetation.

A view from the Yatra Trail of tall trees lining the Yatra Trail on the initial ascent from Chandanwari to Pissu Top

From Chandanwari, finally, a narrow path, a trail, started to lead you towards what seemed like insurmountable mountains.

That trail, that path, would lead you out of the outer encroachments of civilization, and all its manifestations, and into the interiors of the Himalayas.

As you traveled down that path, you were not alone. This sacred path, this yatra trail, with a singular goal, had subsumed and guided the thoughts and hopes and wants and needs and prayers of countless in their search for their maker. On this path, the countless were the one and the same. On this path, the physical, the mind, and the spirit, were all in a unison, they were the one and the same. I pay my deepest respect to this holy path.

Essentially, the Himalayan Journey began here at Chandanwari. There was another billboard at the edge of Chandanwari, detailing the nature of this, the Shri Amarnath Ji yatra trail. This was the time and place to do a last minute inventory of your readiness. You took stock of your equipment, the weather, and your intent and determination. All was in place. Thus, all prepared, all ready, all hopeful, in prayer, one passed by this billboard, and continued on down the yatra trail, towards the next milestone, which was, Pisu Hill Top.

This segment of thc yatra trail was essentially one long climb. Also, on this segment of the yatra trail, one encountered the steepest trail segments of the trek. The distance from Chandanwari to Pisu Hill Top was only 2 miles. In the process of this 2 mile ascent over numerous switchbacks, one gained 2000 ft., that is, going from Chandanwari at an altitude of 9500 ft, to the top of Pisu Hill, at a height of 11500 feet.

The yatra trail from Chandanwari to Pisu Hill Top initially negotiated a path through a covering of trees along the mountain foot hills. The dense coverage of trees, seemingly standing as sentinels to the mountains beyond, kept you guessing about

After the last of the switchbacks, the Yatra Trail arrives at the top of Pissu Top

the nature of the trail ahead. You knew that beyond this curtain of trees was a different world. You strained to look up at the mountains that were now enormous walls in front you.

Somehow, the trail would find a way to take you to the top of these mountains. Along the trail you found a companion, a stream, commonly known as Sheshnag stream.

A view of the last of the zig-zag swithchbacks ascending to the top of Pissu Top

The trail and the stream kept each other company as you continued your ascent up to Pisu Hill Top. You would stay in the company of Sheshnag stream, even after reaching Pisu Hill Top, till you reached the source of the stream. Sheshnag stream originated from a glacial lake named Sheshnag lake. After reaching Pisu Hill, Sheshnag lake would be the next milestone.

As the trail to Pisu Hill Top continually gained in altitude, the air seemingly got thinner and thinner.

The yatra trail continued, the ascent continued, and the trail left behind started to fade into a larger panorama of an enormous alpine mountainous landscape.

A view from the top of Pissu Top of the valley below while looking towards Pahalgam

As you continued towards Pisu Hill Top, you approached a series of switch backs. These switch backs posed to be the bulk of the concentrated high grade on this segment of the yatra trail. The zig-zagging trail, climbing the side of the mountain, finally reached the top of Pisu Hill.

Reaching the Top of Pisu Hill was a pronounced stage of the yatra. Here, a feeling of attainment was already felt. One was well into the yatra. It reflected a stage in a person's life, when and where you knew you had come a long way, and also knew that this would be a point of anchor for the rest of one's existence.

A view from the top of Pissu Top of the valley below while looking towards Chandanwari and Pahalgam

A view from the top of Pissu Top of the Alpine valley below and the Arctic terrain ahead on the Yatra Trail

This process was now undoable. That presence on top of Pisu Hill was indelible and euphorically marked in your very being.

The top of Pisu Hill offered a view of the grand mountain side that was left behind. This was the last vantage point on the trail where one could look at the scope of the alpine countryside below. Also, this was the only point on the yatra trail were there was still a sense of connection between the starting point of Pahalgam, and here, this vantage point on Pisu Hill Top. There you stood, as an observer, perched on top of Pisu Hill. The view of the vastness of the mountainous countryside that was left behind filled the horizon. The tall trees of the terrain below looked like patches of green color, more like a painted canvas landscape, than the enormous trees that they were.

In this seamless view, stretching from the top of Pisu Hill to the horizon left behind any distinction in the scape of this view seemed more a distinction of characteristics, and possibly of a unique perspective, rather than in essence. The view, you, all, seemed connected; it was all a common presence.

Reflecting on your purpose, you turned to visually survey the yatra trail that lay ahead. There, ahead of you, was the yatra trail continuing to Shri

Amarnath Ji. The trail ahead dramatically contrasted with the trail left behind. That which was left behind was alpine, and that which was ahead of you was the outskirts of an arctic mountainous frontier. There you stood on the boundary between the two contrasting realities, in a reflective silence.

Still, there was a sublime unison in all that was perceptually different. That which you were leaving behind and that which was ahead, and you, were still of the same creation, same reality. Also, you, your inner universe and your outer universe, seemed only to have subjective distinctions. The outer views, the inner thoughts, were more of a reflection of the same meditative process, than that of activities of explicit thoughts and observations. In this meditative process, you found yourself lost and found, again and again and again. A sort of a balancing process between the parts and the whole started to engulf you.

In an awareness of the parts, the Perspectives and perception of the particulars, all could be discernable as separate and independent and of it's own nature. In the reality of the perspectives and particular, you were physical and finite, there were trees, and mountains, and streams, and all the infinite combinations of physical and mental. Yet, a sublime synthesis, a divine union of all perspectives and all particulars was self evident, as all was of the same creation, and by the same one creator. All was the one and the same, a miracle of creation, to behold. Thus, leaving no room for hesitance or doubt, in such a reflection, the distinction between the thoughts and things started to fade. An awareness of oneness, a wholeness, a completeness, became inescapable.

It took a great effort to detach yourself from the phenomenal views and perceptions of Pisu Hill Top, and continue the journey. This journey was a yatra, a yatra, and something seeded within you knew what to do next. Thus, the yatra continued.

Thus, over this six mile segment of the yatra trail, from Pisu Hill Top to Sheshnag lake, the Shesnag stream, often predictably, then often unpredictably, kept one company. The ribbon of a trail and the Sheshnag stream, contained within the shouldering mountains, was one's Himalayan corridor for this part of the Yatra.

One of the characteristics of this trail was that the scenery across the horizon changed at almost every bend of the trail. As you approached Sheshnag lake, snow capped mountains started to peek above the lower mountains. As you progressed, eventually, around the last bend of the trail, Sheshnag lake started to partially come into view.

A View from the top of Pissu Top towards Chandanwari and Pahalgam below.

## Holy Maṇḍūkya Upanishad, Verse 2: Revelation

Herein, Verse 2 of the Holy Maṇḍūkya Upanishad became the object of meditation—both the realization and the lived reality of the Yatri on the Yatra Trail.

## Holy Maṇḍūkya Upanishad, Verse 2:
## Realizations on the Yatra Trail

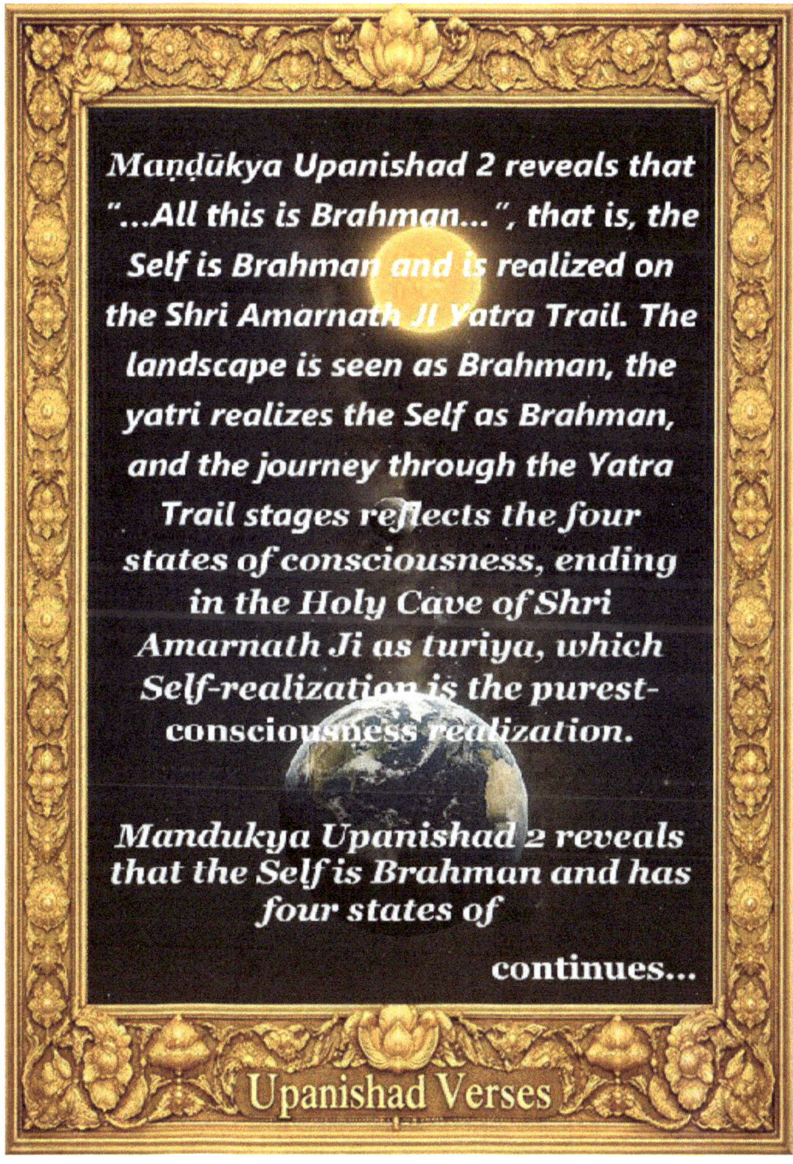

## Holy Maṇḍūkya Upanishad, Verse 2: Realizations on the Yatra Trail

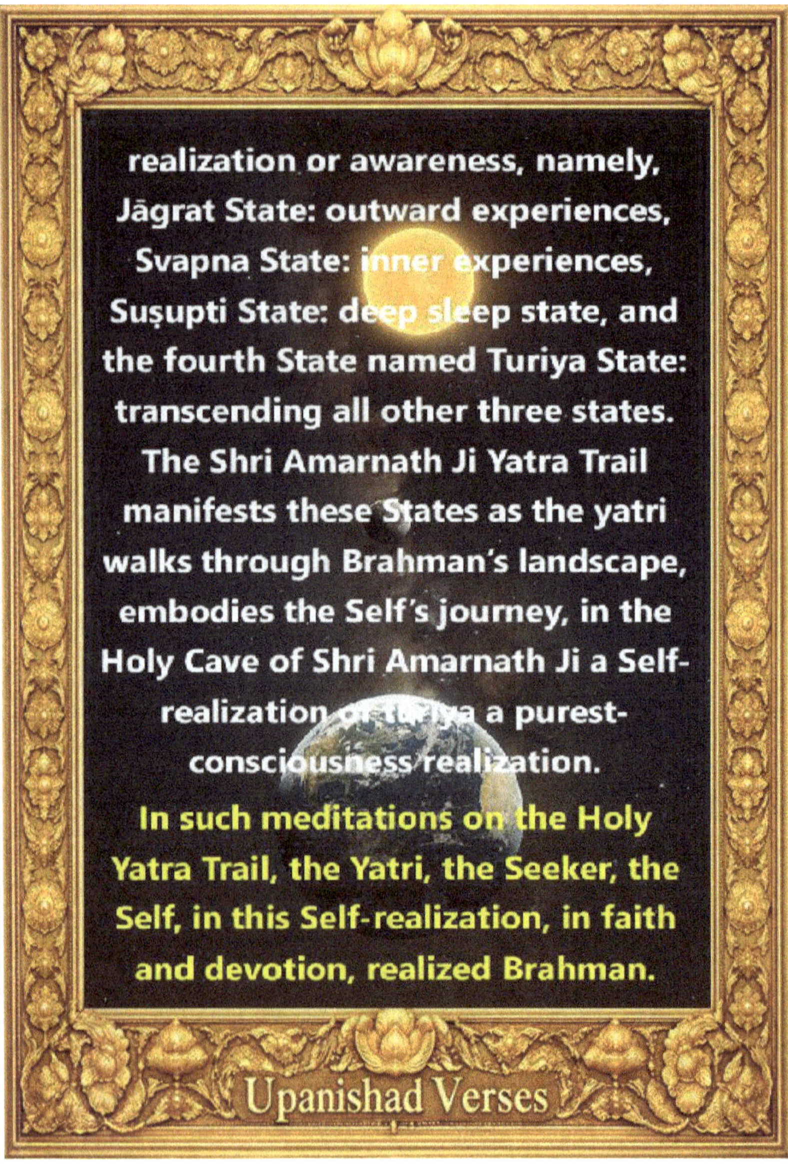

# YATRA TRAIL SECTION 3:
# PISSU TOP TO SHESHNAG LAKE YATRA:

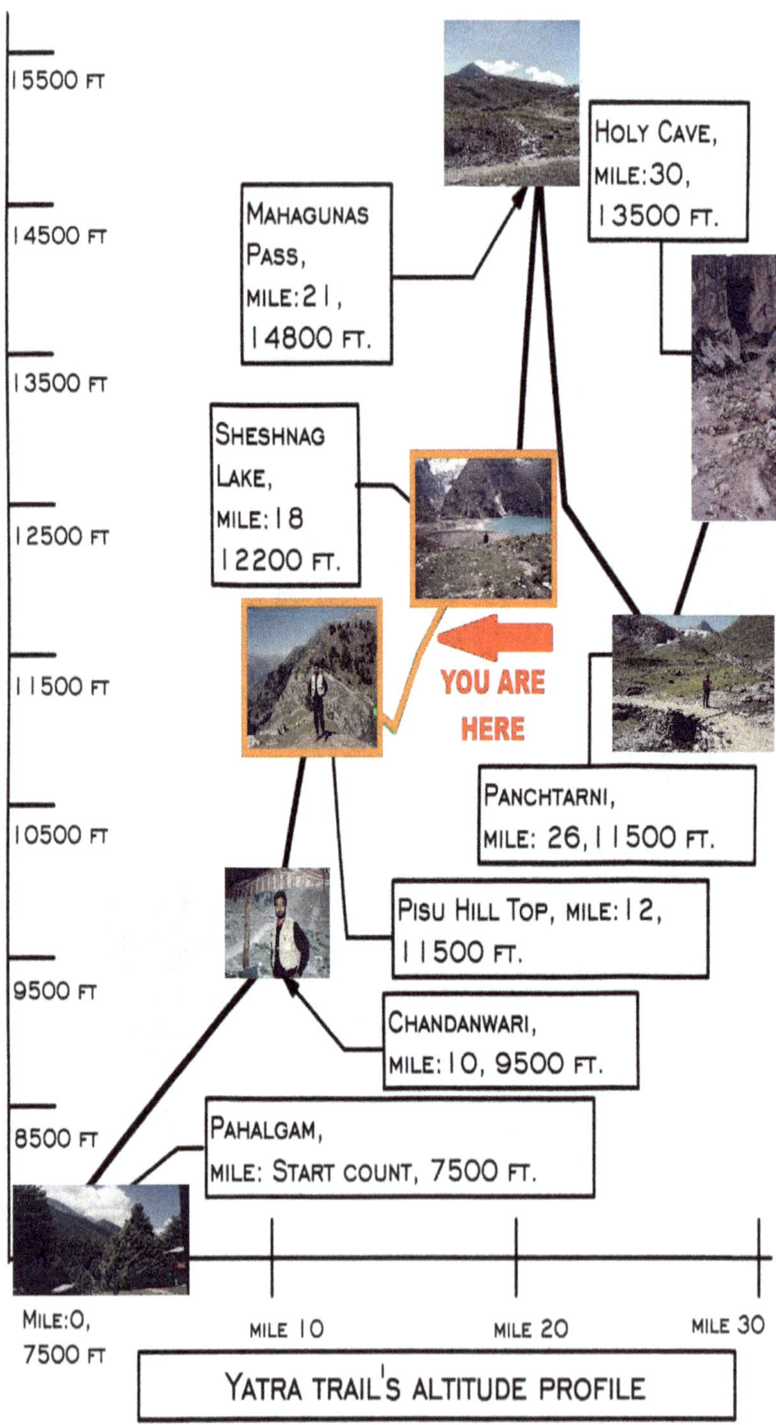
15500 FT
14500 FT
13500 FT
12500 FT
11500 FT
10500 FT
9500 FT
8500 FT
MAHAGUNAS PASS, MILE:21, 14800 FT.
HOLY CAVE, MILE:30, 13500 FT.
SHESHNAG LAKE, MILE:18 12200 FT.
YOU ARE HERE
PANCHTARNI, MILE: 26, 11500 FT.
PISU HILL TOP, MILE:12, 11500 FT.
CHANDANWARI, MILE:10, 9500 FT.
PAHALGAM, MILE: START COUNT, 7500 FT.
MILE:0, 7500 FT
MILE 10
MILE 20
MILE 30
YATRA TRAIL'S ALTITUDE PROFILE

## Terrain Characteristics:

## Pissu Top to Sheshnag Lake:

**Environment:** High alpine meadows and glacial lake basin.

**Area features:** the Sheshnag Lake area is classic alpine, with turquoise color glacial lake, surrounded by high peaks, no trees, mostly grass, shrubs, and rocks.

A view from the Yatra Trail on the way from Pissu Top to Sheshnag Lake with shelters along the Yatra Trail

A view while travelling from Pissu Top to Sheshnag Lake on a wide ascending Yatra Trail with Shelters along the Yatra Trail

The yatra trail from Pisu Hill Top, at 11,500 ft, to Sheshnag lake, at 12,200 ft, over a distance of 6 miles, stayed in the company of Sheshnag stream.

Both the trail and the stream meandered along, as mountain peaks on both sides contained this idle path.

Sheshnag stream was a familiar companion on this part of the yatra. In the stillness of the mountains, the stillness of the enveloping sky, you and the stream seemed the only ones on a journey.

A view from the Yatra Trail, on the way from Pissu Top to Sheshnag Lake, along the descending Sheshnag Stream

Your purposes were taking you up to Sheshnag lake, and Sheshnag stream having left Sheshnag lake, was destined for the valley below. Sheshnag stream, in it's decent down the mountains, would take on many moods and personalities.

A view from the Yatra Trail from Pissu Top to Sheshnag Lake, adjacent to the Sheshnag stream waterfall, with snow patches along the banks of the descending Sheshnag stream

A view of the Yatra Trail while travelling from Pissu Top to Sheshnag Lake, with horses grazing, by the Yatra Trail, adjacent to a waterfall of the descending Sheshnag Stream.

A panoramic view from the ascending Yatra Trail, while travelling from Pissu Top to Sheshnag Lake, and also, a view of the descending Sheshnag Stream, as the Sheshnag Stream travels towards Chandanwari.

At some places, the Sheshnag stream, had chiseled out deep ravines, andoften disappeared out of sight from one's vantage point on the trail, and yet, the ear could often confirm its presence. The trail at times skirted at the edges of these ravines and one's pulse quickened as the shear depth of the ravine came into view.

The stream, at places, was a narrow and fast gushing stream of water. Then at places, the stream would widen out and flowed placidly.

Then again, at times, the stream became more of a hurtling rapid, bouncing off the rocky features of the ravine, as it hurriedly descended down the mountainous terrain to reach the awaiting alpine lands below.

Looming high above the lake, snow capped mountains formed a wall behind the lake.

The emerging lake, and the snow capped mountains over the horizon, both competed for one's full attention. The suspense of what was ahead, as this Himalayan panorama unfolded, saturated one's focus.

Soon enough, as you progressed, the full majesty of the Shesnag blue-green lake covered the horizon, and towering above the lake was a backdrop of enormous Himalayan galactic peaks.

The massive peaks allowed their glacier water to flow into the lake, and crystal clear skies enveloped this Himalayan drama.

The trail itself was on a wide-open shelf, high above the lake. On that shelf, on that worldly stage, you were surrounded by a spectacularly choreographed artistry of nature. Standing silently on that stage, you humbly and respectfully, reveled in this miracle of creation. This shelf, this stage above the lake, was also a playground for the mountain winds. As you stood there, immersed in that universe, the winds raced all around you, and seemingly touched all that there was. All seemed connected. Again, this was a self-evident affirmation of the connectivity and the oneness of it all. After such reflections, in that state of being, it became difficult to distinguish the "**you**" from the "**rest**".

The yatra continued.

A view from the Yatra Trail of the Yatra Trail approach to Sheshnag Lake, as the Yatra Trail arrives from Pissu Top.

View from a shelf above Sheshnag Lake, with views of glacial streams pouring into the lake from the mountains above.

View from a shelf above Sheshnag Lake, with views of glacial streams pouring into the lake from the glacial mountains above.

A view of glacial mountains above and behind Sheshnag Lake, that feed their glacial streams into Sheshnag Lake.

A timeless moment while sitting on the terrain shelf above Sheshnag Lake with a panorama of glacial mountain peaks filling the horizon behind Sheshnag Lake.

A panoramic view of Sheshnag Lake from the Yatra Trail.

From the Yatra Trail, a view of the glacial mountains behind the Sheshnag Lake grounds.

A view from the Yatra Trail of Sheshnag Lake and the Sheshnag Glacial Peaks in the background.

A view of Sheshnag Lake from the Yatra Trail with Sheshnag Glacial Streams feeding into Sheshnag Lake.

## Holy Praśna Upanishad, Verses 2.6, 6.5: Revelation

Herein, Verses 2.6 and 6.5 of the Holy Praśna Upanishad became the object of meditation—revealing themselves as both the realization and the lived reality of the Yatri on the Yatra Trail.

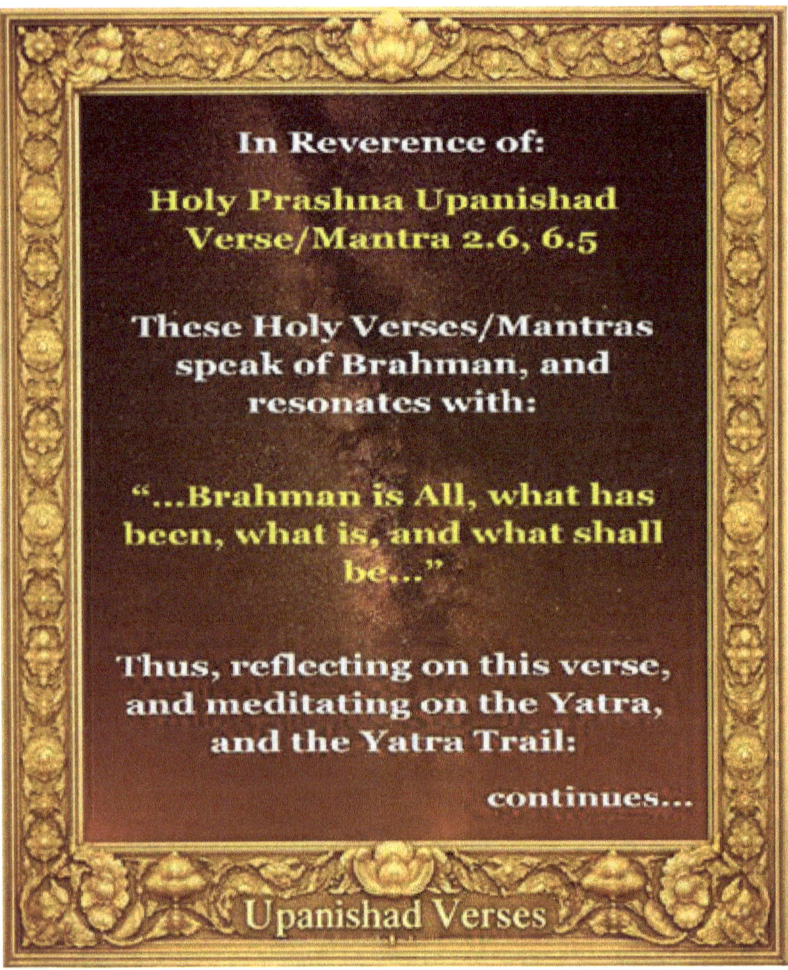

## Holy Praśna Upanishad, Verses 2.6, 6.5
## Realizations on the Yatra Trail

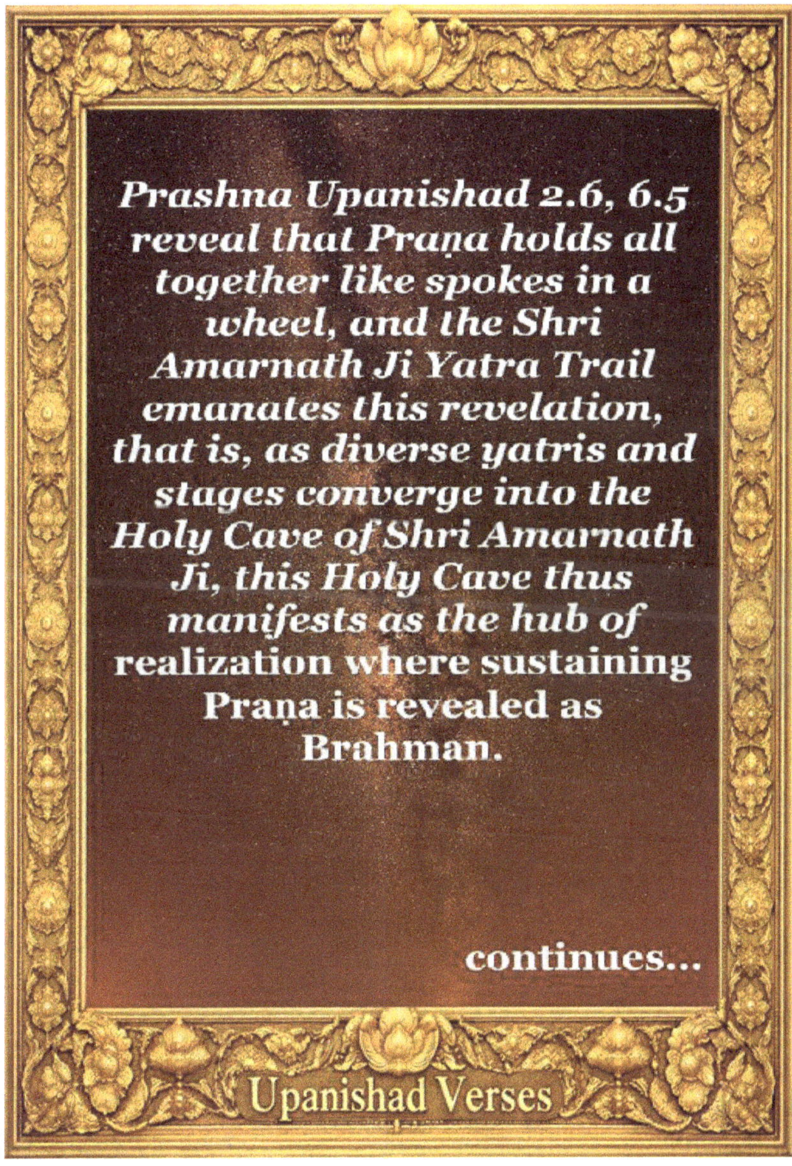

## Holy Praśna Upanishad, Verses 2.6, 6.5
## Realizations on the Yatra Trail

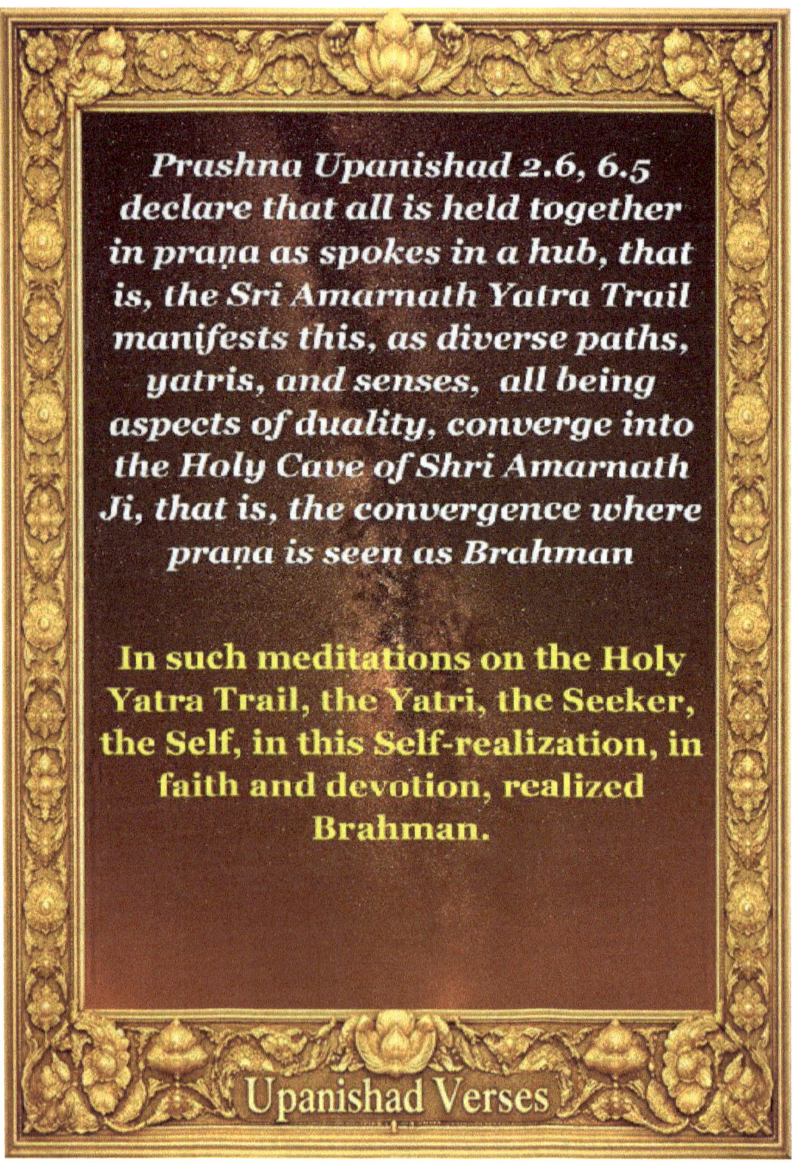

# YATRA TRAIL SECTION 4: SHESHNAG LAKE TO MAHAGUNAS PASS YATRA:

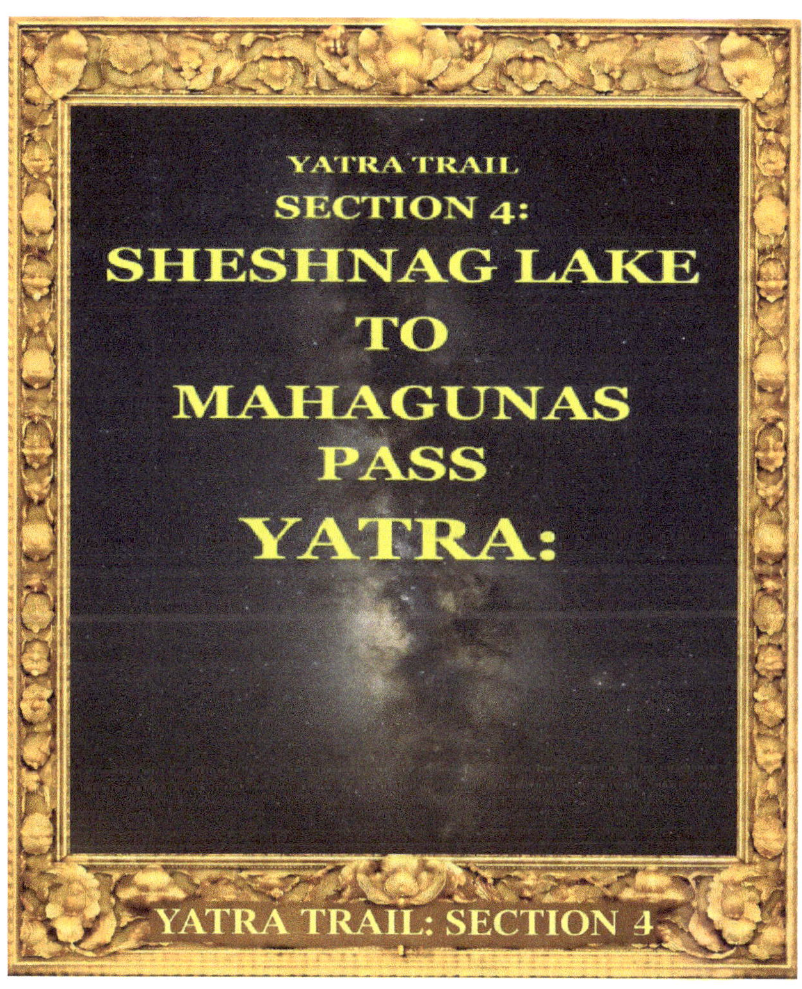

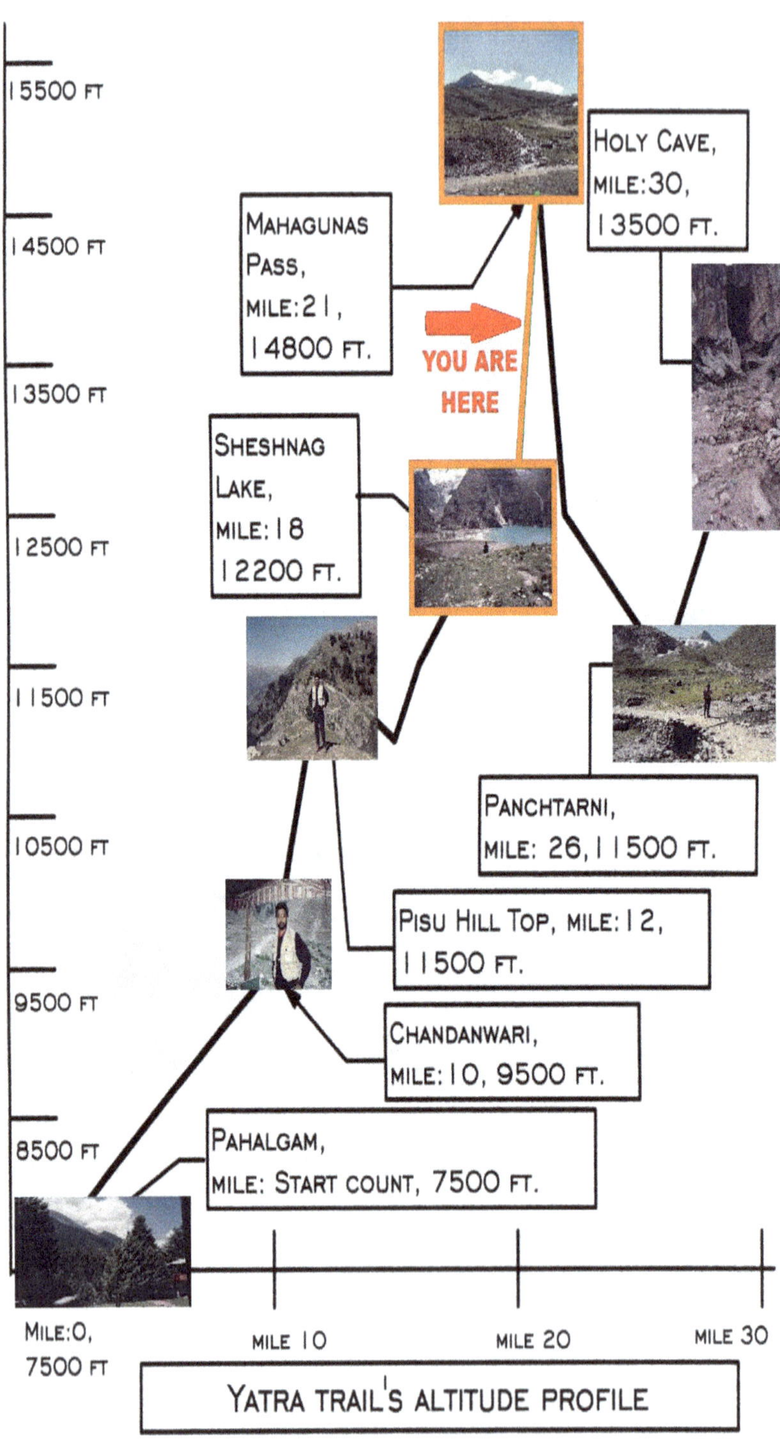
15500 FT
14500 FT
13500 FT
12500 FT
11500 FT
10500 FT
9500 FT
8500 FT
HOLY CAVE, MILE:30, 13500 FT.
MAHAGUNAS PASS, MILE:21, 14800 FT.
YOU ARE HERE
SHESHNAG LAKE, MILE:18 12200 FT.
PANCHTARNI, MILE: 26, 11500 FT.
PISU HILL TOP, MILE:12, 11500 FT.
CHANDANWARI, MILE:10, 9500 FT.
PAHALGAM, MILE: START COUNT, 7500 FT.
MILE:0, 7500 FT
MILE 10
MILE 20
MILE 30
YATRA TRAIL'S ALTITUDE PROFILE

## Terrain Characteristics:

## Sheshnag Lake to Mahagunas Top:

**Environment:** Upper alpine zone (near snow line)

**Area features**: steep ascents, scree, snow patches even in summer, glacial melt streams. Vegetation is minimal—mostly moss, lichens, and hardy grasses.

The Yatra of
reverence
and awareness
continues...

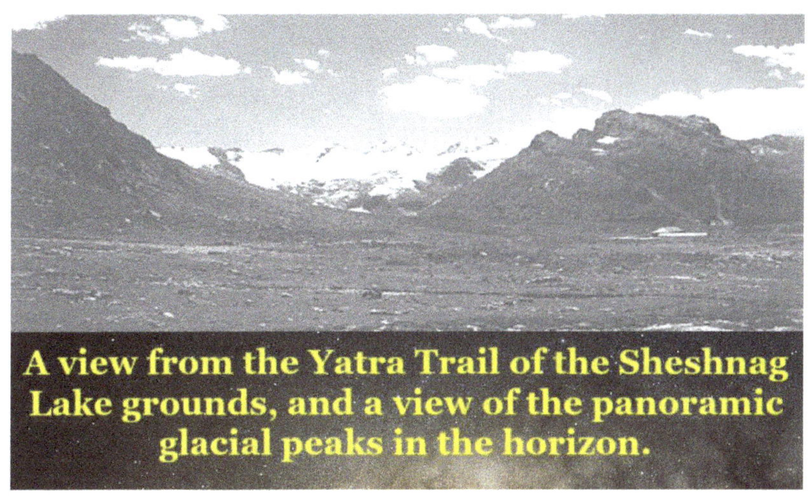

A view from the Yatra Trail of the Sheshnag Lake grounds, and a view of the panoramic glacial peaks in the horizon.

As you progressed towards Mahagunas Pass, leaving Sheshnag Lake became a gradual process. The yatra trail heading towards Mahagunas Pass, for quite a duration, stayed in the company of the overshadowing glacial peaks of Sheshnag Lake.

A view of Sheshnag Lake's glacial mountains as seen from the ascending Yatra Trail while travelling between Sheshnag Lake to Mahagunas Top.

A view from the Yatra Trail ascending from Sheshnag Lake to Mahagunas Top, along with a view of Sheshnag glacial mountains in the in the distant horizon.

A view from the Yatra Trail ascending from Sheshnag Lake to Mahagunas Top, along with a view of Sheshnag glacial mountains and snow covered peaks in the distant horizon.

The trail from Pisu Hill to Sheshnag Lake had been a casual walk along the meandering Sheshnag stream.

Now, however, the trail from Sheshnag Lake to Mahagunas Pass took the casualness out of the trekking effort. On this segment of the yatra trail, there was a relentless ascent. The thin atmosphere at this high altitude, made this the most physically demanding segment of the yatra trail's hiking effort. The trail went from 12200 ft at Sheshnag Lake, to 14800 ft at Mahagunas Pass, over a distance of three miles. That being a gain of 2600 ft, in the progressively thinning atmosphere, made it explicitly clear to you that you were well within the interiors of the Himalayas. Mahagunas Pass was the highest point on the yatra trail.

On the trek to Mahagunas Pass, the trail gradually ascended and the surrounding terrain reflected this ever so increasing altitude. There was a lessening of the grassy covering around the foot of the mountains. The mountains were, now, hues of earthy brown and shear rock surfaces. The tops of some of these mountains were laden with snow, defying the summer season.

This unyielding nature of the Himalayas, perhaps not very inviting to living things, was bold and pure and uncompromising.

From Sheshnag Lake, a narrow ribbon like Yatra Trail, along the mountain slopes, ascends towards Mahagunas Top

Just as the lower Himalayan mountain region offered one a promise of alpine beauty, perhaps, the rugged nature of Mahagunas Pass was a clear indication of the forbidding character of the Himalayas, as one proceeded deeper into its interior.

Again and again, you looked back at the towering glacial peaks that overshadowed Sheshnag Lake. In this mountain corridor, the world was simplified. There was just that which was ahead of you on the trail, and that which you left behind. The shepherding mountains on both sides of the yatra trail did not leave room to go astray. Thus, as you ascended, and also, as you stopped to rest, you surveyed the world behind, and the world ahead.

A view from the Yatra Trail, as it arrives on Mahagunas Top: Mahagunas Pass is a Mountain Pass that connects Sheshnag Lake to Panchtarni.

A view fromYatra Trail arriving from Sheshnag Lake, as it passes The Mahagunas Top highest Yatra Trail traversed area, and as the Yatra Trail descends towards Panchtarni.

**From the top of Mahagunas Top, with shelters adjacent to the Yatra Trail, the Yatra Trail mapped out a gradual descending route towards Panchtarni.**

Slowly, after much anticipation and trekking effort, the very top of the Mahagunas Pass arrived. Cold winds at the top of the Pass could be heard and felt as they channeled through and around the adjoining mountain features. Here, at the top of the Mahagunas Pass, the temperature suddenly dropped, and cold brisk air nudged and swayed you.

From the top of Mahagunas Pass, one could see the descending trail on the other side of Mahagunas Pass, in the direction of Panchtarni. The view towards Panchtarni looked like a three dimensional road map.

This road map sketched out a descending and a winding trail headed down the Pass. The yatra trail, well contained within the adjoining mountains, disappeared into the horizon.

This Himalayan road map was clear and compelling; one blissfully followed it.

**The Yatra Trail descends from Mahagunas Top, on a gradual winding slope, towards Panchtarni.**

A view from the Yatra Trail looking towards the Sheshnag Glacial Peaks, as the ascending Yatra Trail approaches Mahagunas Top.

## Holy Isha Upanishad, Verses 6, and 7: Revelation

Herein, Verses 6 and 7 of the Holy Isha Upanishad became the object of meditation—at once the realization and the lived reality of the Yatri on the Yatra Trail.

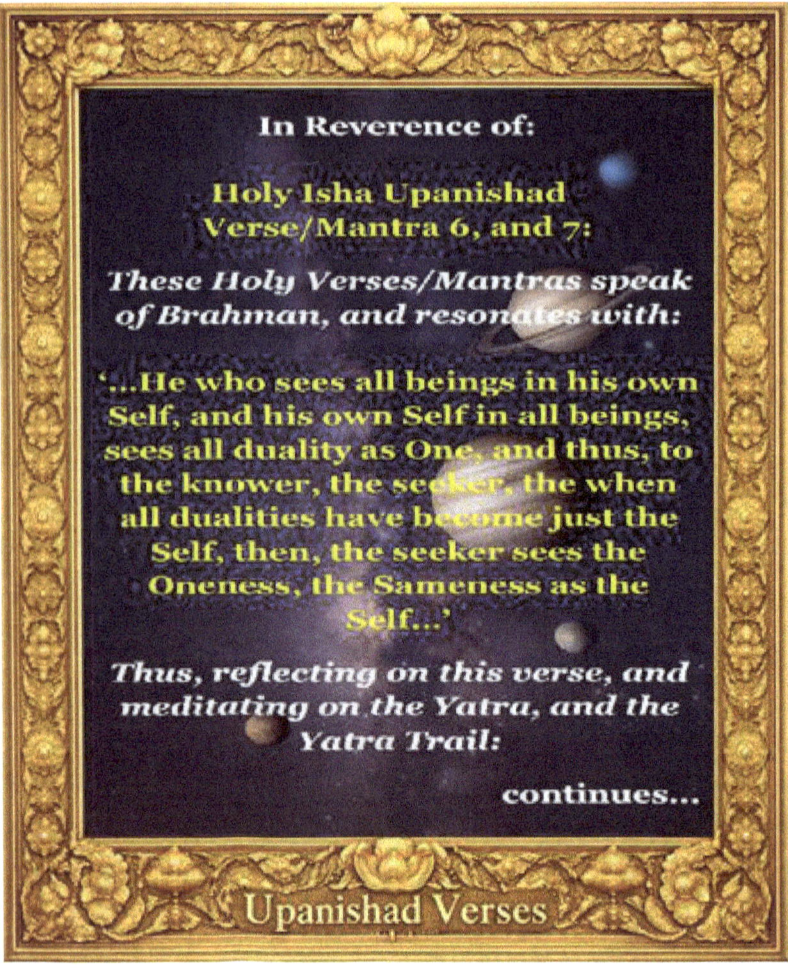

## Holy Isha Upanishad, Verses 6, and 7 and Realizations on the Yatra Trail

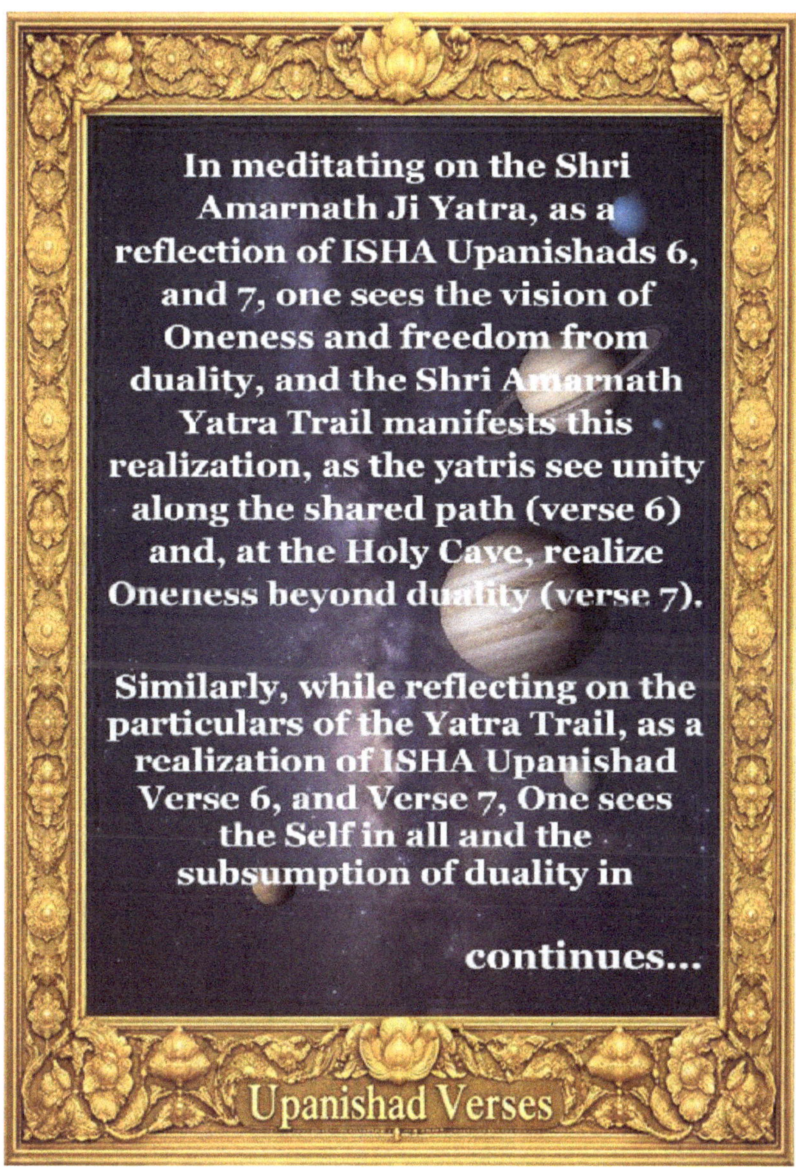

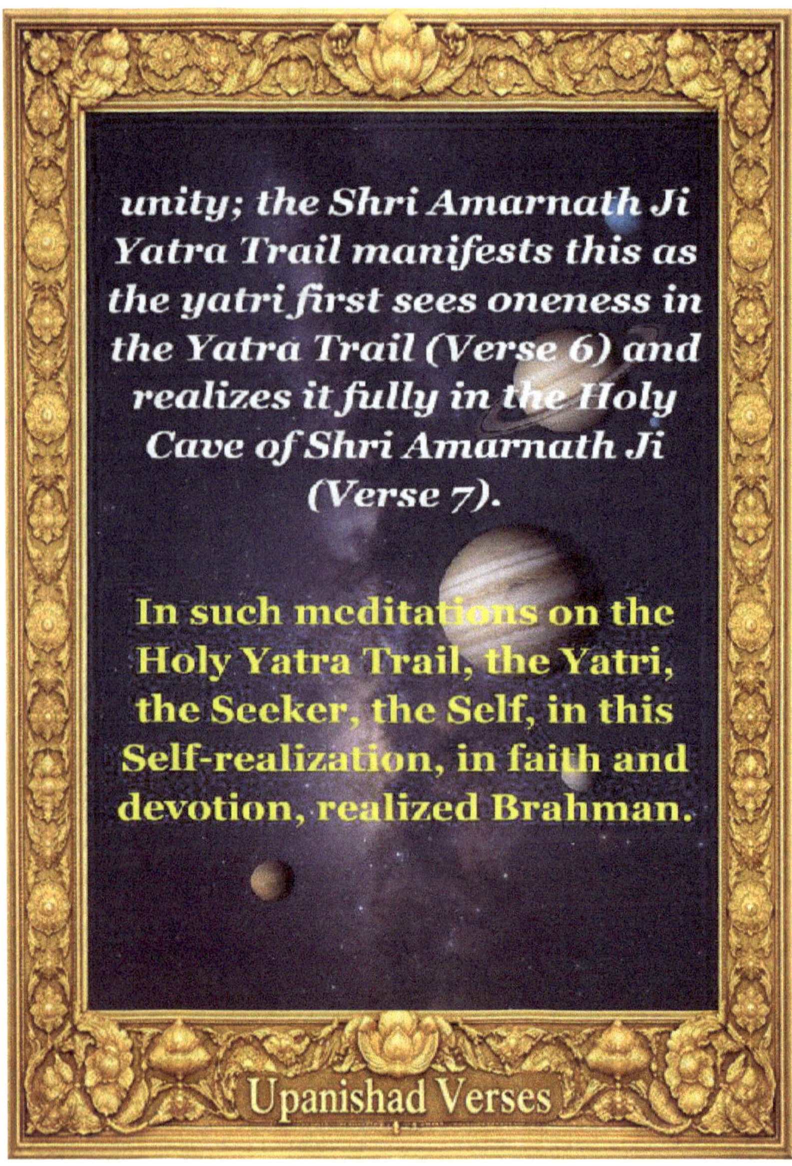
*unity; the Shri Amarnath Ji Yatra Trail manifests this as the yatri first sees oneness in the Yatra Trail (Verse 6) and realizes it fully in the Holy Cave of Shri Amarnath Ji (Verse 7).*
In such meditations on the Holy Yatra Trail, the Yatri, the Seeker, the Self, in this Self-realization, in faith and devotion, realized Brahman.
Upanishad Verses

# YATRA TRAIL SECTION 5: MAHAGUNAS TOP TO PANCHTARNI YATRA:

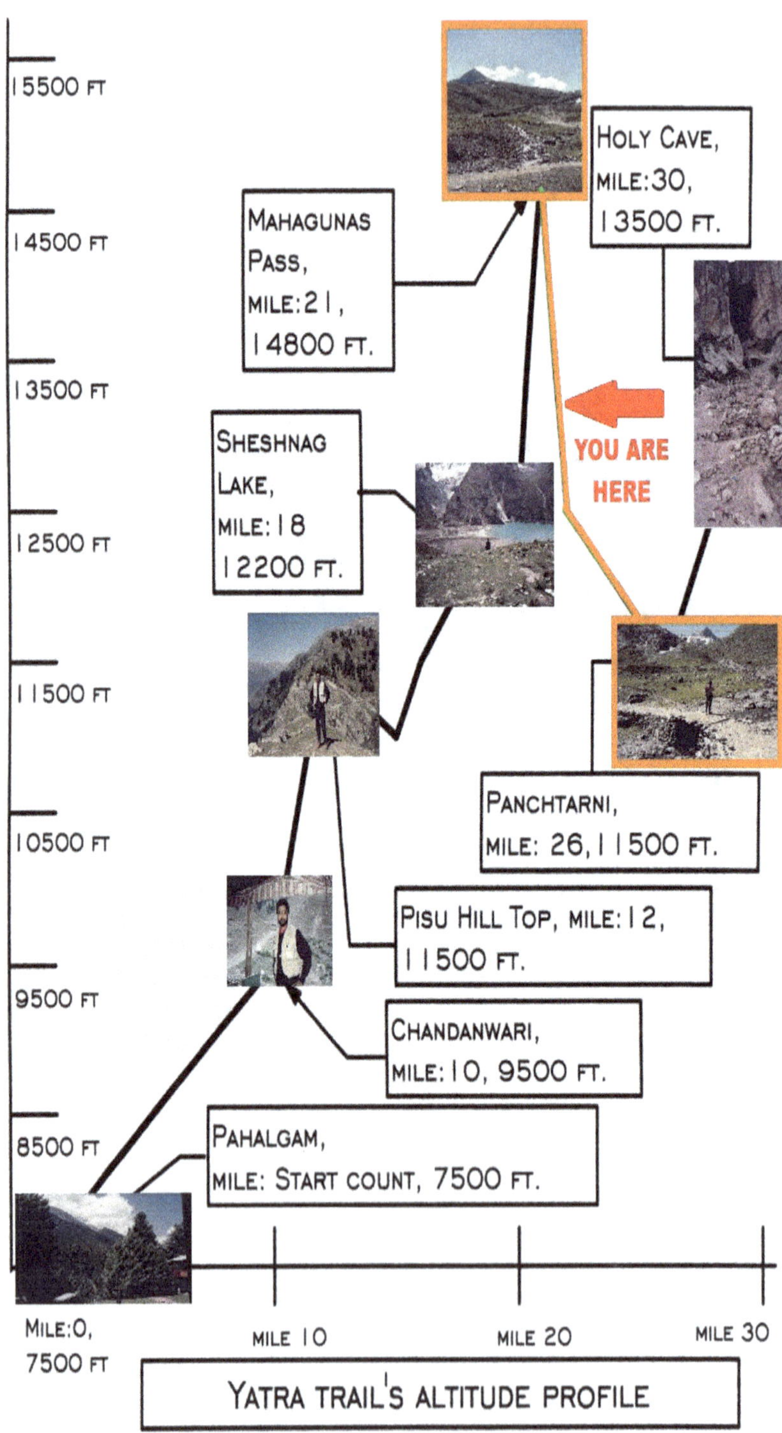
15500 FT
14500 FT
13500 FT
12500 FT
11500 FT
10500 FT
9500 FT
8500 FT
Holy Cave, mile:30, 13500 ft.
Mahagunas Pass, mile:21, 14800 ft.
Sheshnag Lake, mile:18 12200 ft.
YOU ARE HERE
Panchtarni, mile: 26, 11500 ft.
Pisu Hill Top, mile:12, 11500 ft.
Chandanwari, mile:10, 9500 ft.
Pahalgam, mile: Start count, 7500 ft.
Mile:0, 7500 ft
mile 10
mile 20
mile 30
Yatra trail's altitude profile

## Terrain Characteristics:

## Mahagunas Top to Panchtarni:

**Environment:** Upper alpine zone (near snow line)

**Area features:** steep ascents, scree, snow patches even in summer, glacial melt streams. Vegetation is minimal—mostly moss, lichens, and hardy grasses and arctic tundra conditions: cold, windy, barren.

Your journey down Mahagunas Pass didn't need much momentum. After the arduous ascent to Mahagunas Pass, the tendency here was to almost run down towards Panchtarni. The gradually descending yatra trail was an invitation to quickly be at Panchtarni. So, in a child-like exuberance, you walked, you ran, you skipped down the trail. What other life's experience could compare with running and dancing down a 14,800 ft mountain Pass. It was an experience beyond compare. You knew this moment and carefreeness would be an everlasting bliss in your life.

Panchtarni was about 5 miles from the top of Mahagunas Pass. You descended from 14800 ft, at the top of the Pass, to 11500 ft at Panchtarni.

The terrain from Mahagunas Pass to Panchtarni maintained a consistency in character that could be described as alien to most of our experiences. It was as if one was walking in a landscape that had been untouched by time. The standard of time, as seen by us mortals, had little meaning in these Himalayan formations.

From the top of Mahagunas Top, with shelters adjacent to the Yatra Trail, the Yatra Trail mapped out a gradual descending route towards Panchtarni.

**A view from the Yatra Trail from the top of Mahagunas Top, as the Yatra Trail heads to Panchtarni, and renders a physical map of a meandering and a gradually descending Yatra Trail.**

The Yatra Trail from Mahagunas Top, arriving at the Panchtarni meadow like grounds, with a view of water streams across the foreground, and towering mountain peaks in the background.

Yatra Trail from Mahagunas Top, arriving into Panchtarni, as the panoramic view of Panchtarni fills the horizon, as seen from the Yatra Trail.

The trail weaved its way through these bold mountains. The mountains towering along both sides of the trail alternated between hues of gray rock formations, to layering of brown sedimentary deposits; all this, recording the signatures of seasonal Himalayan history. Despite such formidable terrain condition, alongside the trail, and at the lower foot-hills of the mountains, there existed green grassy vegetation, seeming to defy the rules of nature.

One could only admire this phenomenon called life, and how it relentlessly asserted itself on this planet. One could almost visualize the emergence of life on this planet by this Himalayan example.

A panoramic view of Panchtarni, while standing on the vast grassy meadow like grounds in Panchtarni, cradled by towering mountains.

Progressing down the trail, finally, Panchtarni appeared at the horizon. Panchtarni was situated on a flat bed of land and was largely encircled by towering peaks. Across its open facade, streams of water crossed the approaching trail. Crossing of these streams was not a difficult task. At points, the water was at best a few inches above the ground. The trickier parts of the streams had wooden bridges constructed above them.

A view from the Panchtarni grassy grounds, with storm shelters in the foreground, and towards the background, the ascending Yatra Trail starts between the sloping mountain ridges, towards the Holy Cave of Shri Amarnath Ji.

A view from the Yatra Trail in Panchtarni, arriving from Mahagunas Top, with grassy grounds in the foreground, and storm shelters in the distant horizon, and a panoramic background of sheltering mountains.

**A view from the Yatra Trail in Panchtarni, as it crosses shallow streams in places, and bridge structures are a part of the Yatra Trail.**

**The vast flat grounds of Panchtarni, with provisions for a Helipad, with flowing shallow streams, and with a background of sheltering mountains.**

One's arrival into the Panchtarni camp ground was an extremely gratifying experience. Several factors probably contributed to your sense of peace. It perhaps had to do with the knowledge that the journey's end was only 5 miles from here. Also, the flat land, and the sheltering mountain

**In the Panchtarni grounds, a view of the storm shelters situated at the foothills of the mountain range, and along the storm shelters, a view of the Panchtarni Stream bed.**

refuge like appearance of Panchtarni, reassured one's sense of security. Also, the luxury of air richer in oxygen than what was experienced just a few hours ago at Mahagunas Pass was a welcome relief.

**In Panchtarni grounds, a view of the storm shelters in the foreground, and in the background, between the sloping mountain ranges, on the right mountain range, is the Yatra Trail that ascends to the Holy Cave of Shri Amarnath Ji.**

It didn't take much time to get accustomed to Panchtarni. It was as if you were enveloped into yet another self-contained world. The large and flat pasture like grassy campground, protected by the encircling mountains, made you feel at home. This was an unescapable feeling. You did not feel that you were at 11500 feet, and in the interior of the Himalayas. Rather, the wide open, flat, pastoral campground, made you feel that you were in a park like setting of your common experience.

You had come a long distance from Pahalgam. Now, the last segment of the Yatra trail was ahead of you. There was nothing else there now, but to be there.

A view from Mahagunas Top towards Panchtarni of a descending and winding Yatra trail.

A view of Panchtarni's vast grounds from the Yatra Trail's arrival from Mahagunas Top.

## Holy Isha Upanishad, Verse 1: Revelation

Herein, Verse 1 of the Holy Isha Upanishad became the object of meditation—both the realization and the lived reality of the Yatri on the Yatra Trail.

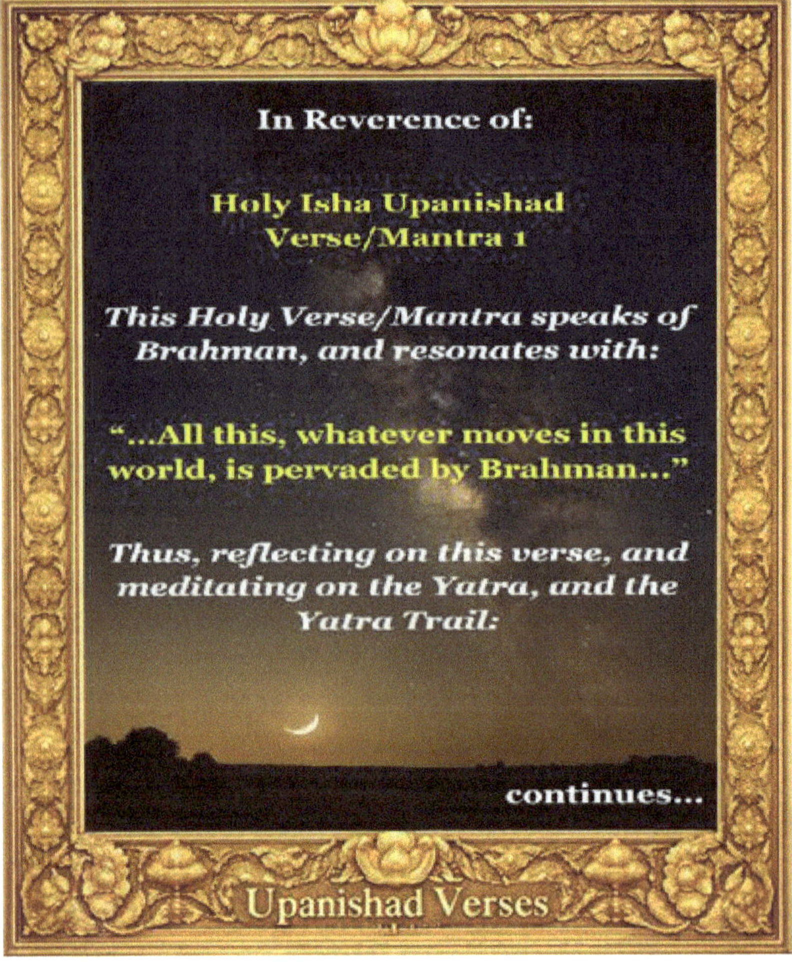

## Holy Isha Upanishad, Verse 1: Realizations on the Yatra Trail

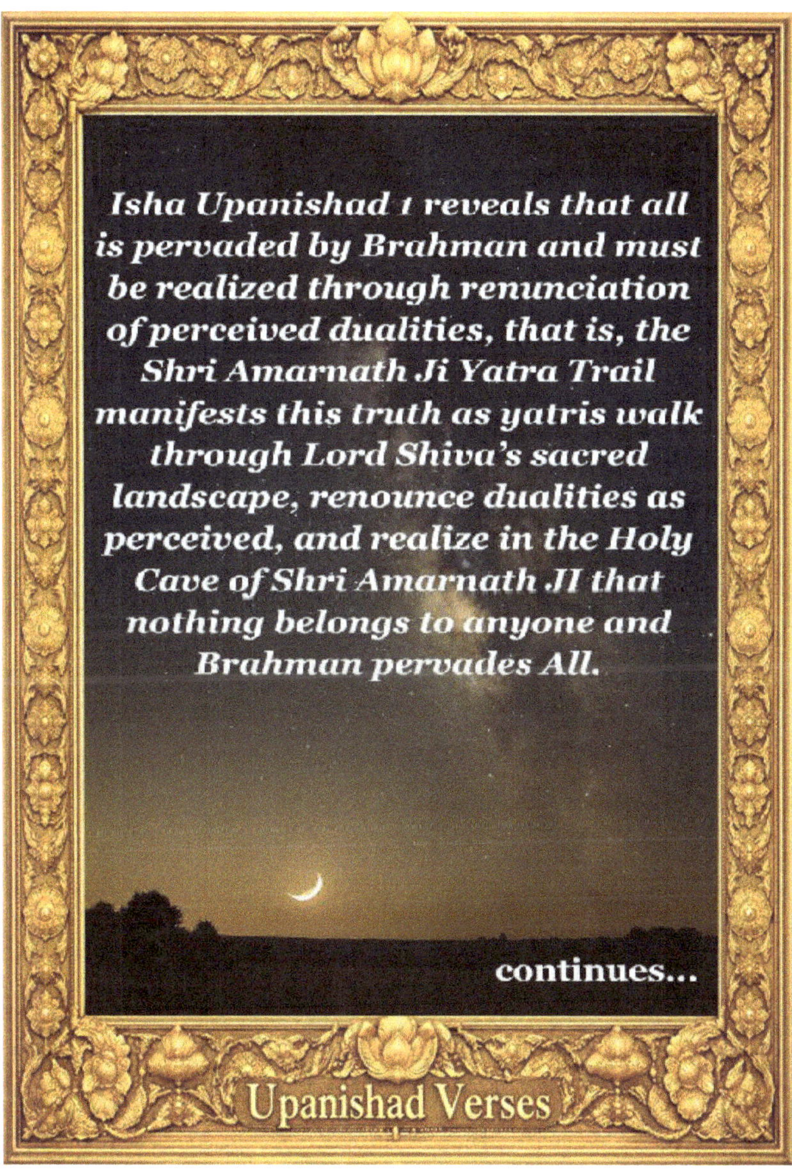

## Holy Isha Upanishad, Verse 1: Realizations on the Yatra Trail

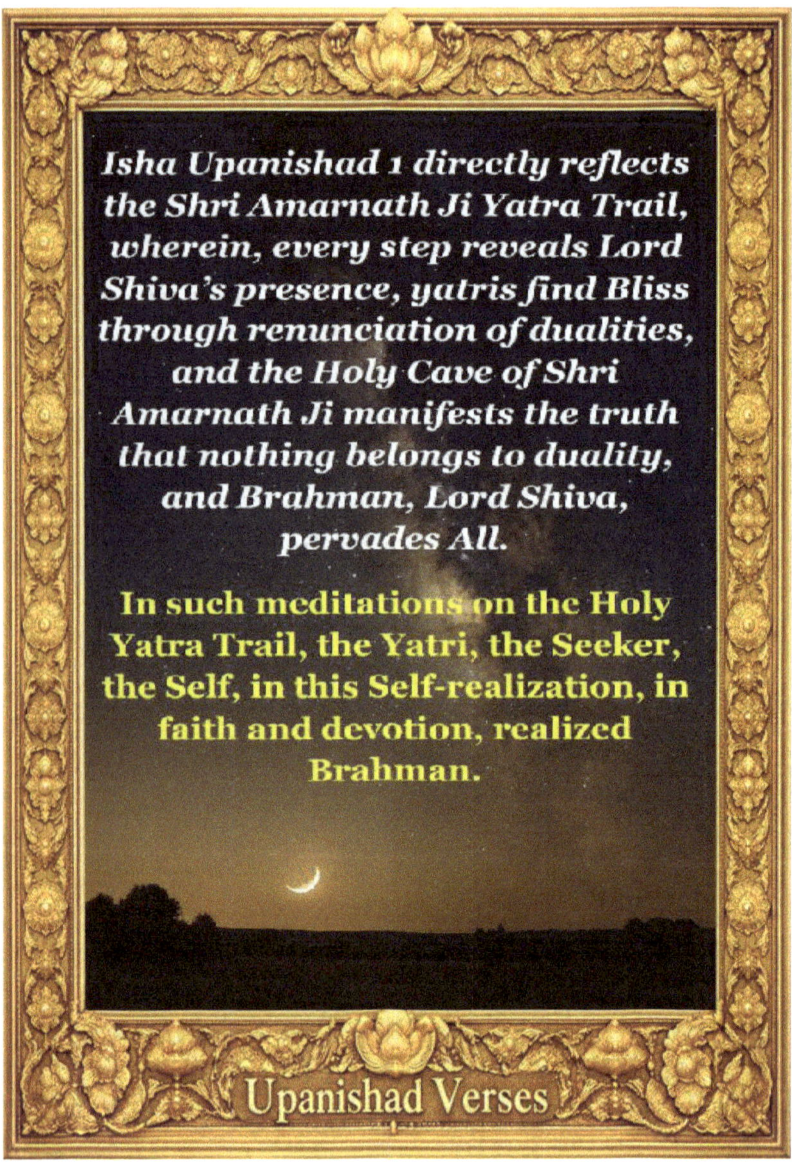

# YATRA TRAIL SECTION 6: PANCHTARNI TO THE HOLY CAVE OF SHRI AMARNATH JI YATRA:

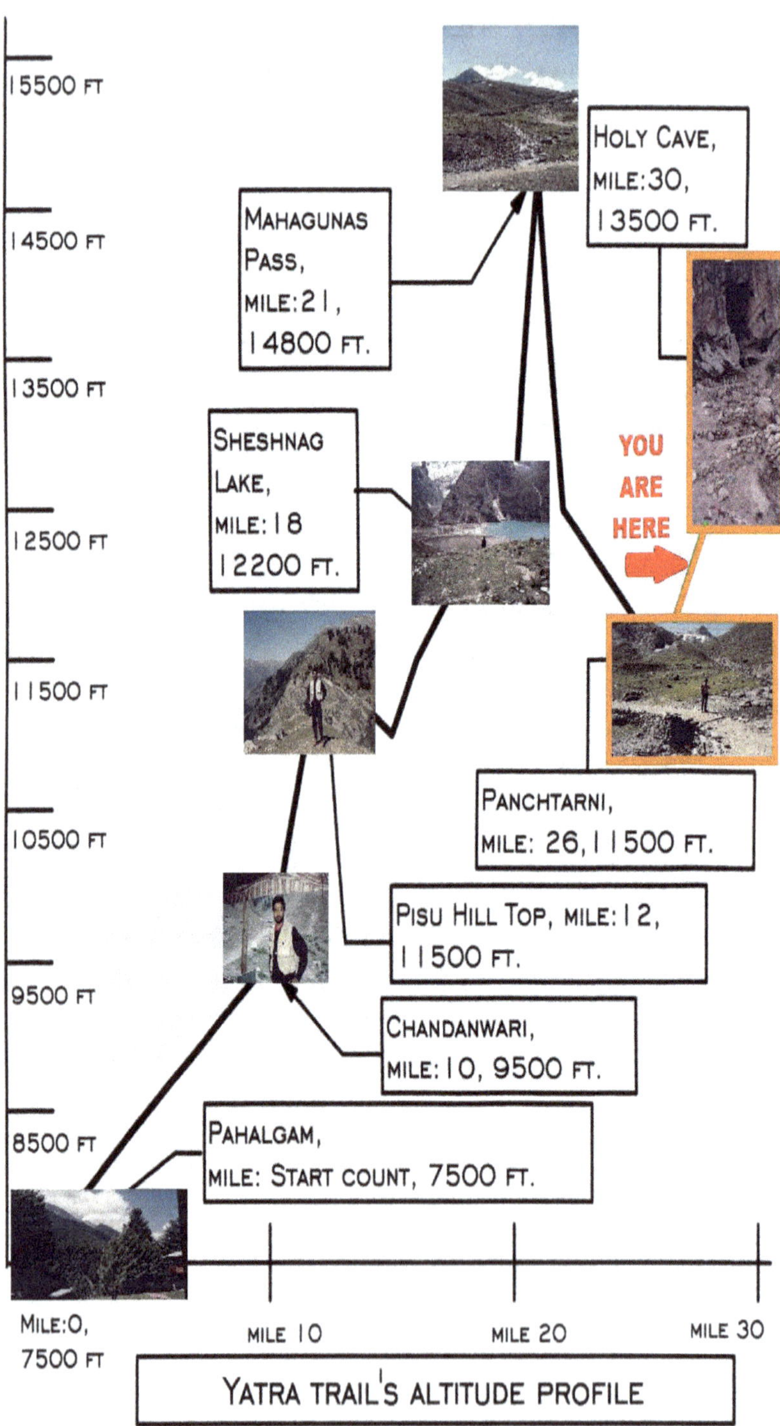
15500 FT
14500 FT
13500 FT
12500 FT
11500 FT
10500 FT
9500 FT
8500 FT
MAHAGUNAS PASS, MILE:21, 14800 FT.
HOLY CAVE, MILE:30, 13500 FT.
SHESHNAG LAKE, MILE:18 12200 FT.
YOU ARE HERE
PANCHTARNI, MILE: 26, 11500 FT.
PISU HILL TOP, MILE:12, 11500 FT.
CHANDANWARI, MILE:10, 9500 FT.
PAHALGAM, MILE: START COUNT, 7500 FT.
MILE:0, 7500 FT
MILE 10
MILE 20
MILE 30
YATRA TRAIL'S ALTITUDE PROFILE

## Terrain Characteristics:

## Panchtarni to Shri Amarnath Ji Holy Cave:

**Environment:** Glacial / Upper alpine zone (near snow line)
**Area features:** rugged moraines, permanent snow patches, icy streams, and the cave itself formed in a glacier-fed valley, and sub-arctic to arctic terrain: high cold desert with snowfields, very thin vegetation, high UV exposure.

The Yatra of
reverence
and awareness
continues...

**The Yatra Trail from Panchtarni, initially adjacent to the Panchtarni stream, ascends along the right mountain ridge, headed to the Holy Cave of Shri Amarnath Ji.**

The Holy Cave is situated in narrow valley, named Amarvati Valley. The last 4 mile segment of the yatra trail would take one from Panchtarni, at an altitude of  11500, to Amarvati Valley, and as such to the Holy Cave of Shri Amarnath Ji. The Holy Cave is at an altitude of 13500 ft.

**A view from the Yatra Trail descending into Amarvati Valley, with snow and ice fields covering the Amarvati Valley. The snow and ice fields also covered the Amarvati Glacial Stream, wherein, the Amarvati Glacial Stream flows along the length of the Amarvati Valley. In this view, The Holy Cave of Shri Amarnath Ji, appears as a distant feature along the left mountain slope of Amarvati Valley.**

From Panchtarni, for a mile or so, the yatra trail steadily climbed and paralleled the forceful Panchtarni stream. Then, the trail steepened and turned into a series of switchbacks, and made it's way along mountainous side walls, heading towards Amarvati valley. The yatra trail ascended for about two-thirds of the way to the Holy Cave, and the remaining portion was a gradual descent into Amarvati Valley.

Soon, on your progression on the yatra trail, around the last of the bends of the yatra trail, on a gradually descending mountainous slope, the long and narrow Amarvati Valley opened up into view.

Snow covered a large portion of the bottom of the valley, and at places, the yatra trail was covered under packed snow. On the bottom of the valley, along the length of the valley, flowed a stream, named the Amarvati. Near the end of the valley, as you faced the open valley, on the left side of the valley, was the Holy Cave.

The yatra trail, largely, paralleled the Amarvati stream. As you progressed in the direction of the Holy Cave, traveling along the Amarvati stream, the trail forced you to cross the long snow fields. A concrete storm shelter was situated a short distance before the Holy Cave. Tall mountains narrowly contained the yatra trail on both sides.

As you progressed, searchingly, you surveyed the mountain features, all the way up to the horizon, for a sign of the Holy Cave. Soon you started to be

**A view from the Yatra Trail, in the Amarvati Valley, as it stays along the Amarvati Stream, heading towards the Holy Cave of Shri Amarnath Ji, that is situated on the left mountain slope, located in the distant horizon.**

aware of a distinct feature on the mountainous wall, on the left side of the valley. This feature became your focal point. This enigmatic focal point, situated at the distant horizon, became all

The Yatra Trail approaches the Holy Cave of Shri Amarnath Ji entrance.

engrossing as you approached it. This focal point, at first, appeared as just a break in the seemingly repeating texture of the mountains along the valley.

Soon, that focal point became resolvable and clear; it was indeed a Cave, the Holy Cave of Shri Amarnath Ji. As you got closer, the magnitude of the Holy Cave became increasingly obvious, as it slowly started to fill most of one's field of view.

Finally, one reached the base of the Holy Cave. The immensity of the Holy Cave overwhelmed the senses. This massive structure elevated above the valley floor, and the trail, was accessible by a long sequence of man made marble steps, that lead up to its entrance. The purity of the Himalayas, and the sanctity of the Holy Cave, formed a sacred union.

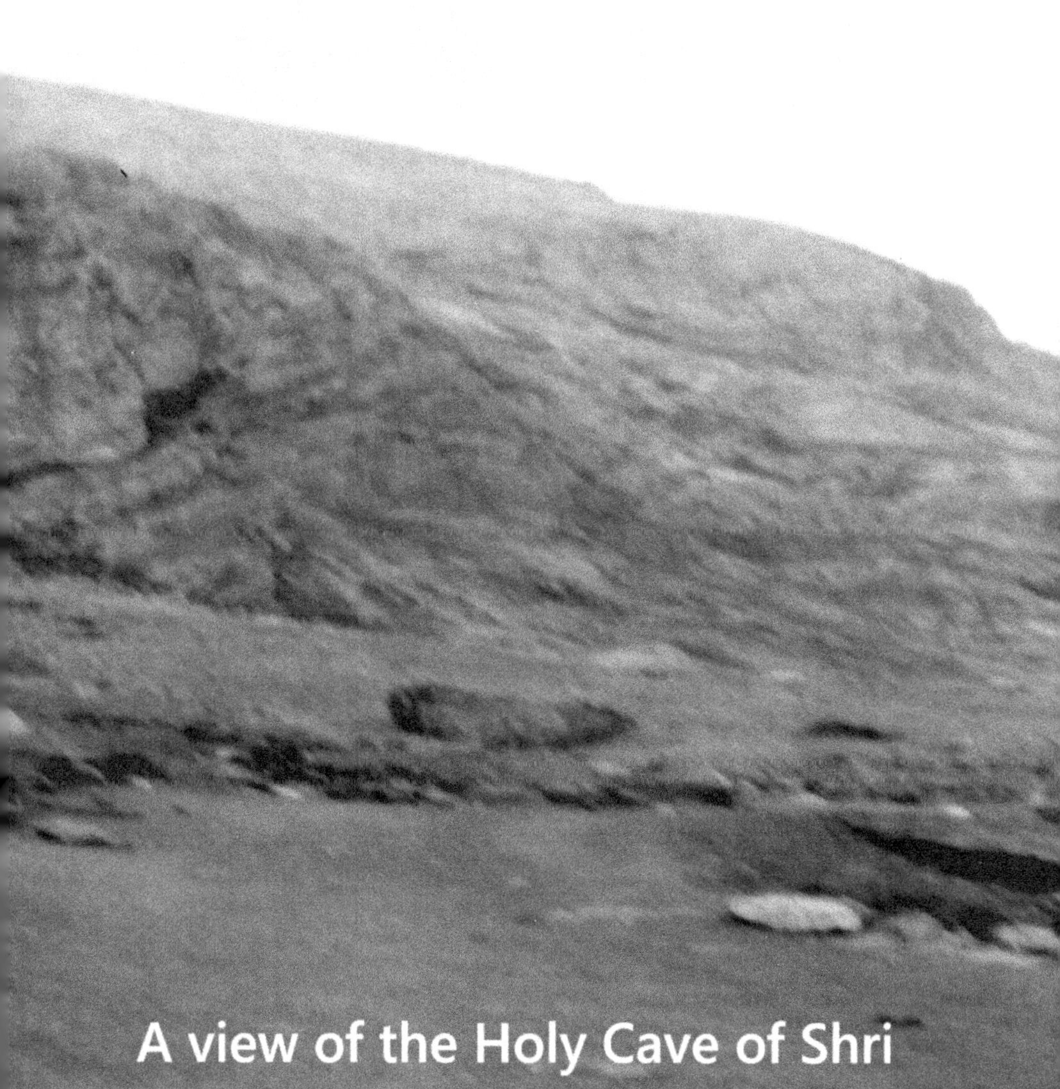

A view of the Holy Cave of Shri Amarnath Ji from the Yatra Trail, from the final Yatra Trail segment of the Holy Yatra.

**In Amarvati Valley, also called the Amarnath Valley, from the floor of the valley, the final ascent of the Yatra Trail, up the mountain slope, to the enterance of the Holy Cave of Shri Amarnath Ji.**

The entrance to the Holy Cave of Shri Amarnath Ji pronounced your arrival, in the form of a Billboard, situated just out side the Holy Cave of Shri Amarnath Ji, affirming your location.

**At the entrance of the Holy Cave of Shri Amarnath Ji, the final steps before the entry into the Holy Cave, are marble steps, that seamlessly connect the Yatra Trail, the Yatri, with the final destination of the Holy Yatra, the Holy Cave of Shri Amarnath Ji.**

As you entered the Holy Cave, the steps leading up to the Holy Cave entrance seemed to become more symbolic than physical. After miles of uneven trail, stepping barefoot onto the cold, smooth, marble steps, and thus into the enveloping Holy Cave, in the shadow of the towering peaks, was an undefinable, surrealistic, and yet a blessed moment. The sight, the feelings, the thoughts were all too difficult to fathom. One was left expressionless. One stepped onto the marble steps very gently. It seemed as if the steps were but a process of elevation, as if one was stepping up from the earthly existence to a higher plateau. After the last of the marble steps, one was there. The journey was complete.

There, here, then, now, forever, we in our deepest devotion perform our obeisance, our deepest respect, our prayer, our puja, to Shri Amarnath Ji, and pray that we all be blessed. Om.

## PART THREE: DARSHAN AT THE HOLY CAVE OF SHRI AMARNATH JI:

Brahman is One, but the seeing of Brahman is many. The Upanishads affirm that realization is not imposed — it is an invitation. One must choose to see.

A few Realizations of selected Upanishads, as personally and selectively interpreted below, collectively, resonates with the personal aspects of a Darshan.

**1. Katha Upanishads realization:**

Only those who turn inward *by choice* see the Self.
Thus: Realization is personal orientation.

**2. Brhadaranyaka Upanishads realization:**

Perception depends on intention and inner disposition.

Thus: Realization is shaped by personal mental stance.

**3. Mundaka Upanishads realization:**

The Self reveals Itself only to the inwardly prepared.
Thus: Realization is conditional and reciprocal.

**4. Chandogya Upanishads realization:**

Brahman is everywhere but seen only by the calm meditator.
Thus: Realization requires personal practice.

**5. Isa Upanishads realization:**

Seekers attain different degrees of vision depending on their path.

Thus: Realization varies among individuals.

Thus, Every one of these Upanishadic passages supports that the darsana (seeing) of Brahman is not automatic, not uniform, not identical for every person — but profoundly personal, arising from one's own inner effort, preparation, purity, intention, and spiritual maturity.

In other words:

Brahman is one — but the seeing of Brahman is many.

The Upanishads themselves say this unambiguously.

As a summary: Upanishadic passages align closely with that idea: that the realization (darsana, "seeing") of Brahman is profoundly personal, arising from one's own disposition, preparation, and insight — not something seen identically or granted universally.

A Personal Darshan, of this Yatra to the Holy Cave of Shri Amarnath Ji, and realization of a personal Darshan is described as follow:

After the Yatra to the Holy Cave of Shri Amranth JI, as my Mother could not travel on this Yatra, I showed My Mother the Photo I took of the Inside of the Holy Cave Of Shri Amarnath Ji, to show my Mother the Image of the Holy Shive Linga of the Ice Formation as an object of our Darshan.

My Mother looked at the photograph with reverence and in her Darshan showed me the Image of Lord Shiva behind the Image of the Holy Shiva Linga also as the object of the Darshan inside the Holy Cave of Shri Amarnath Ji.

After my realization and Darshan of the image of Lord Shiva behind the image of the Holy Shiv Linga, as a miraculous and undeniable observation in the photographic image, my Darshan became a new realization.

Soon enough, I spent time looking, studying, for other such images within the photograph for a similar realization, for a similar miracle.

The images, as comprised in this section, with the applied captions, are shared herein as an effort of such observations, such realizations, such miracles.

It is also realized in this Darshan that the entire Holy Cave of Shri Amarnath Ji is sacred, each stone, each drop of water, the air itself, in the

Holy Cave of Shri Amrarnath Ji is Sacred, and a Darshan.

Thus, without any comments, the following images are shared herein with a spirit of devotion and reverence of a personal Darshan at the Holy Cave of Shri Amarnath Ji. The captions with each respective Image as provided is reflective of a personal Darshan.

Realization of a Darshan of the sacred Shivling in the Holy Cave of Shri Amarnath Ji.

Realization of a Darshan of the sacred Shivling in the Holy cave of Shri Amarnath Ji

A realization of Darshan of
the left side of the Holy Cave
of Shri Amarnath Ji, as
viewed from the front
enterance of the Holy Cave.
HOLY CAVE

A realization of a Darshan of
Shri Ganesh Ji in the Holy
cave of Shri Amarnath Ji
HOLY CAVE

A realization of a Darshan
of Parvati Mata Ji in the
Holy cave of Shri
Amarnath Ji
HOLY CAVE

A realization of a Darshan of
Mahadev Ji (Lord Shiva Ji),
in the Holy Cave of Shri
Amarnath Ji.
HOLY CAVE

A realization of a Darshan of a Tiger Head Ji, in the Holy Cave of Shri Amarnath Ji.
HOLY CAVE

A realization of Darshan of a composite form of Mahadev Ji (Shiv Ji), Tiger Head Ji, Staff Ji, and Nāgarāja Vāsuki Ji, in the Holy cave of Shri Amarnath Ji.
HOLY CAVE

A realization of a Darshan of a composite form of Mahadev Ji (Lord Shiva), Tiger Head Ji, Staff Ji, and Nāgarāja Vāsuki Ji, along with Ganesh Ji and Parvati Mata Ji, in the Holy cave of Shri Amarnath Ji
HOLY CAVE

## Holy Muṇḍaka Upanishad, Verse 2.2.11: Revelation

Herein, Verse 2.2.11 of the Holy Muṇḍaka Upanishad became the object of meditation—both the realization and the lived reality of the Yatri upon the Yatra Trail.

## Holy Muṇḍaka Upanishad, Verse 2.2.11:
## Realizations on the Yatra Trail

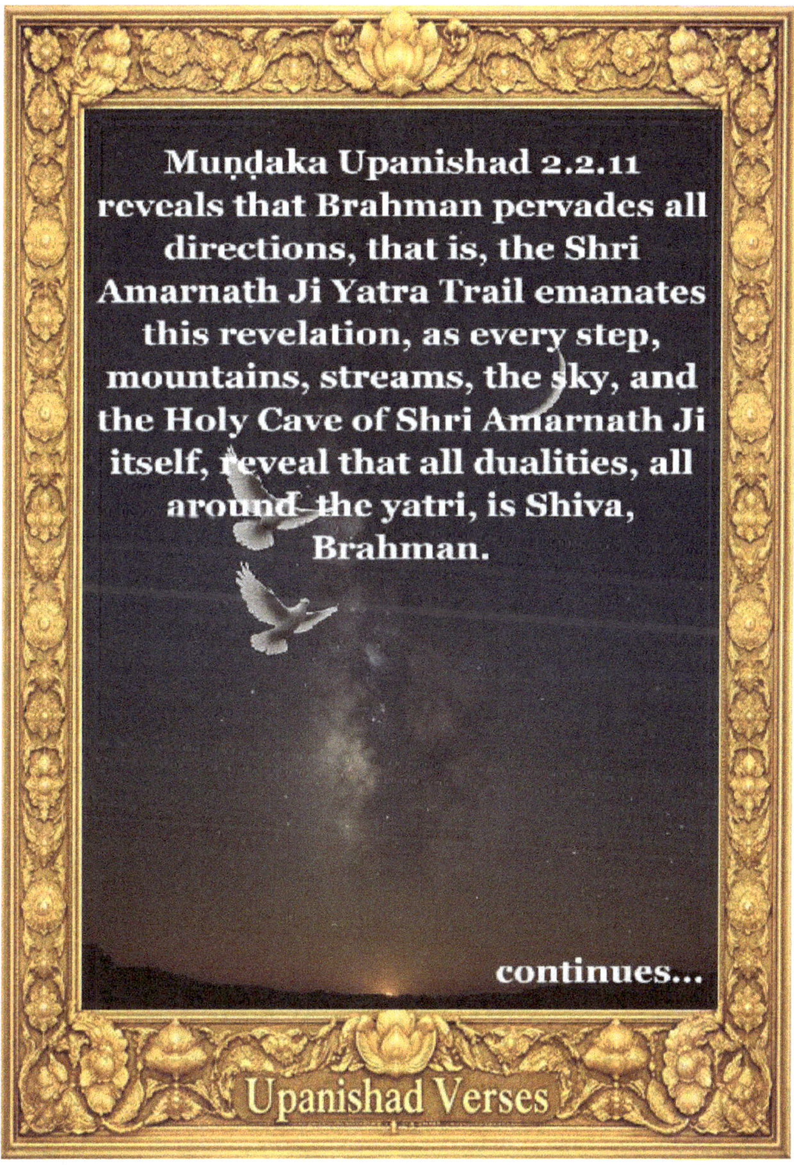

## Holy Muṇḍaka Upanishad, Verse 2.2.11: Realizations on the Yatra Trail

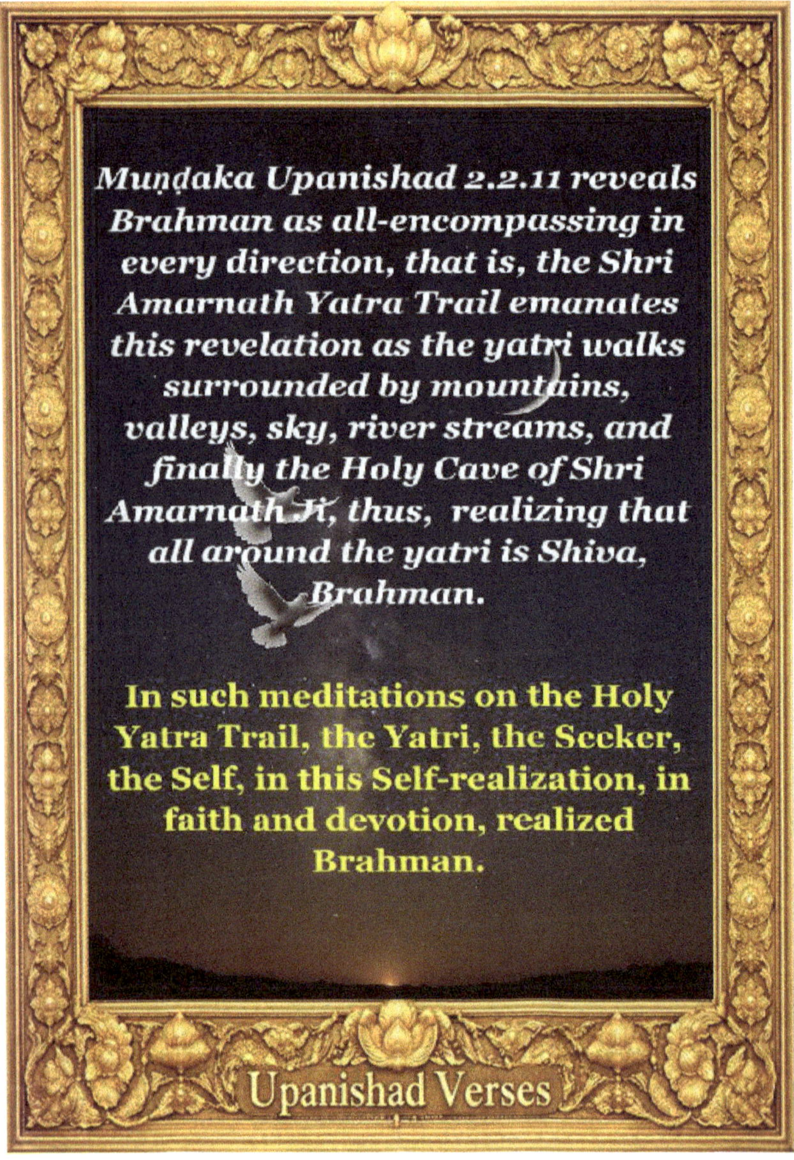

# PART FOUR: REFLECTIONS OF THE YATRI, THE SEEKER, AND THE HOLY YATRA:

As the physical body embarks on a yatra, so do the mind and the spirit, and the thoughts, and the reflections that are imbued within the being.

These characteristics of the being, collectively and solemnly observe and reflect on the experience of the yatra. As the senses behold the spectacular Himalayan miracle of the Shri Amarnath Ji yatra, the mind and spirit, in devotion and prayer, celebrate this miracle. Thus, a yatra begins, in the spirit of respect and prayer and devotion and celebration of Shri Amarnath Ji.

## Holy Taittirīya Upanishad, Verse 2.1: Revelation

Herein, Verse 2.1 of the Holy Taittirīya Upanishad became the object of meditation—both the realization and the lived reality of the Yatri on the Yatra Trail.

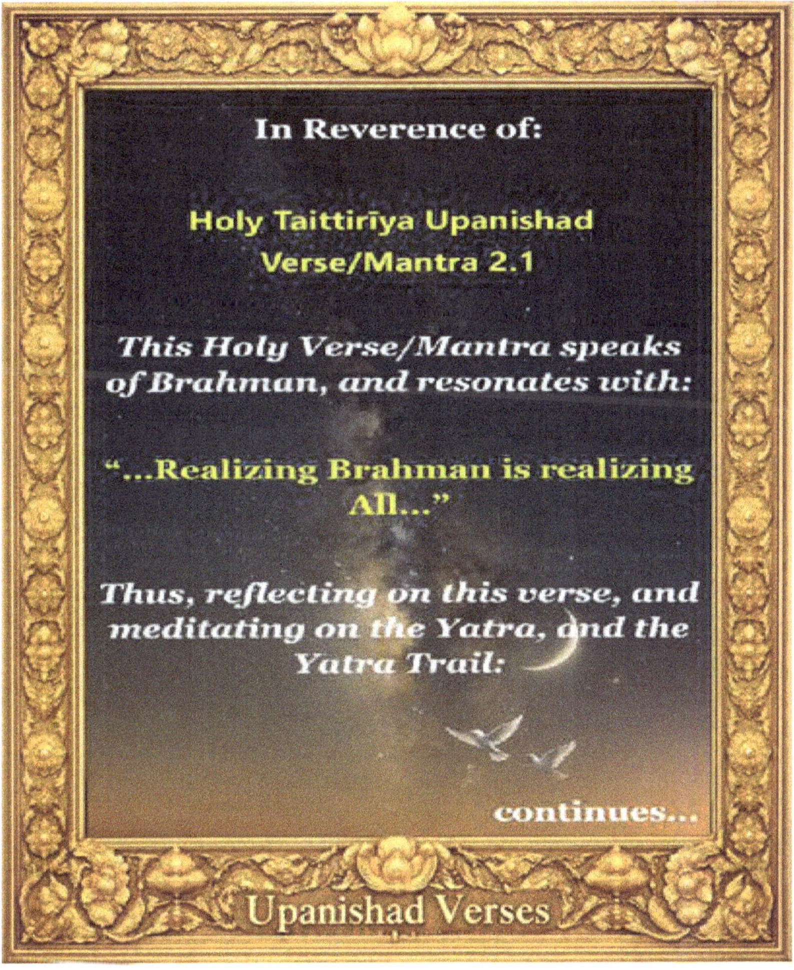

# Holy Taittirīya Upanishad, Verse 2.1: Realizations on the Yatra Trail

## Holy Taittirīya Upanishad, Verse 2.1: Realizations on the Yatra Trail

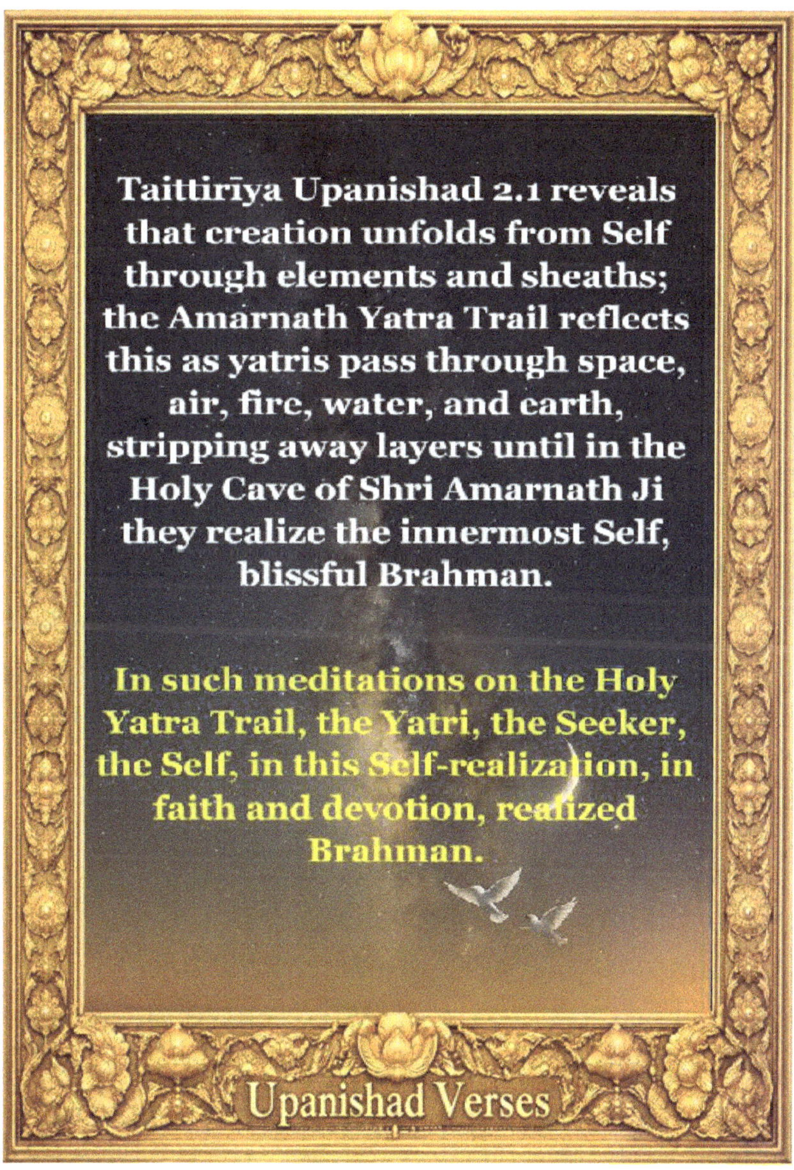

The holy yatra trail, when surrendered to the senses, became a well-defined path on the ground with mountains and sky to contain it. The physical mountains would contain and focus the path of the yatra trail into the direction of the Holy Cave. The mountains of the mind, the mountains of the ever-wandering thoughts, also kept the mind focused forward, towards the Holy Cave, as this was a clear path, a clear hope, a clear prayer, and a clear answer.

It was a strange feeling to notice how things simplified and resolved as you progressed on the yatra trail.

Your observations and your cognition and your spirit started to form into an amalgam, a oneness, an amalgam of a state of knowing. The questions of life, questions of thoughts and things, started to transform into answers of a subsuming of the particulars and perspectives of thoughts and things. In this process, the particulars and perspectives of thoughts and things started to seek a definition of completeness, a definition of a simplicity, a definition of wholeness, a oneness. This wholeness and the completeness was the creation, which in some way encompassed all the particulars and the perspectives of creation. Thus, all was reduced to a creation and a creator, and all was sacred. There was no imaginable argument against that. It was perfect, that was the perfection, that was the completeness, that was the wholeness, that was the simplicity, that was the truth, that was the one and the all, and the same, and the one, that was truth, that was the final reality.

This sacred reality of the creation and the creator was the object of your prayers, your reverence, your devotion, your yatra. This amalgam of you was here on this yatra trail, in this wholeness of creation, to do a yatra, a yatra to the abode of the creator and re-creator of all.

## Holy Aitareya Upanishad, Verse 3.1.3: Revelation

Herein, Verse 3.1.3 of the Holy Aitareya Upanishad became the object of meditation—both the realization and the lived reality of the Yatri upon the Yatra Trail.

## Holy Aitareya Upanishad, Verse 3.1.3:
**Realizations on the Yatra Trail**

## Holy Aitareya Upanishad, Verse 3.1.3:
## Realizations on the Yatra Trail

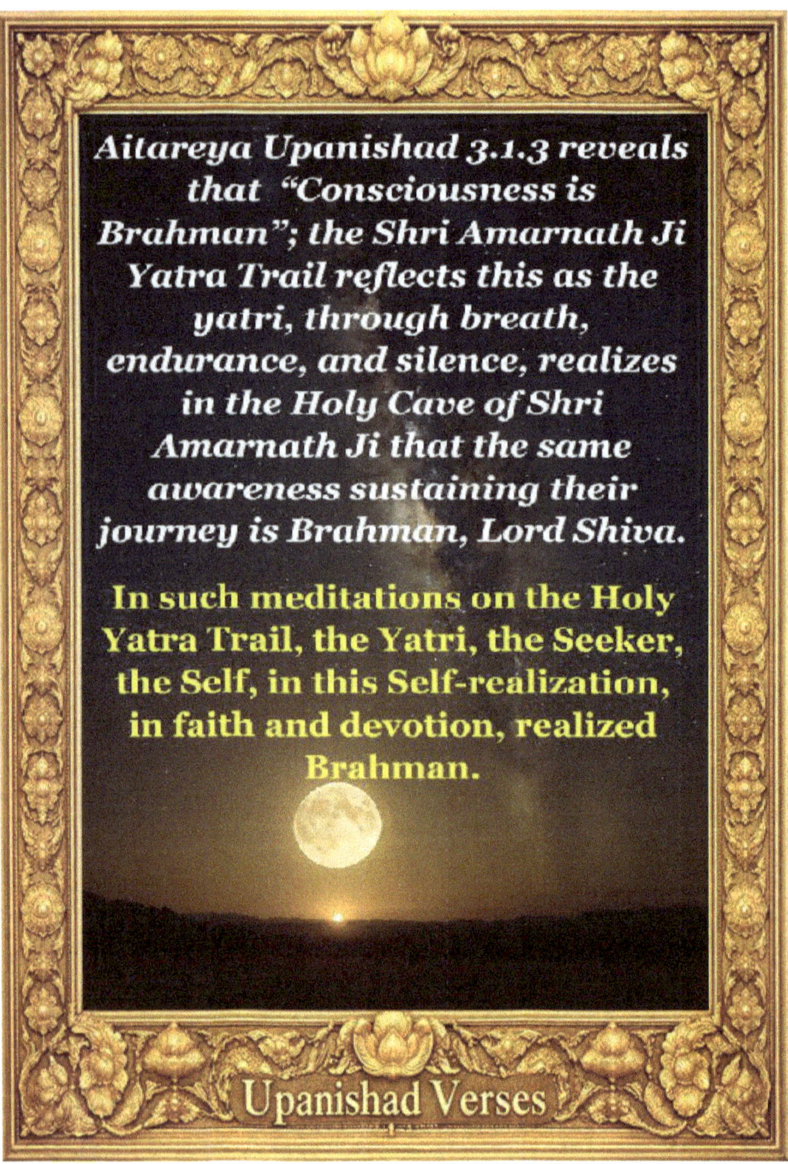

I pay my deepest respects to Shri Amarnath Ji, the abode of the creator and re-creator of creation.

Thus, you knew the truth. The many perceived manifestations of reality, the particulars, were more a matter of reflection and perspective, and not of multiple truths.

**Thus, one reality, one truth, one whole: Self-evident Brahman.**

From the perceptually trivial, to the unfathomable, thus must be the nature of reality. In this self-reflection, perhaps, there was a self-realization. This is all introspective, and perhaps retrospective in thought as well, yet, the Being, the Self, in its need to know, found such self-reflections to surface again. On this yatra trail, the mind found its answers in such reflections. In these answers was a peace that settled the wandering and the wondering mind. Thus, all that was physical, was sensible to the senses, all the thoughts, now settled, were meaningful to the mind, and all was perfect and a miracle to behold.

To the spirit, it was a matter of faith and devotion, it just knew, it was self-evident, it was in a solemn prayer and celebration, in Bliss.

Thus, also, you understood your existence. The myriad of earthly actions and interactions and attachments were now in their true perspective.

Now you knew, what was Maya, this Maya that was a reality of perception, of dualities. This Maya of the physical and the mental. This Maya of attachments. This mosaic of Maya, of the physical, the mental, the attachments, and your life thus lived and spent, was now, to you, suddenly, clear. Your evolutionary search for truth and answers in this realm of Maya, this quest by the means of a search for the meaning of a meaning of a meaning, was endless. You had even made bargains with your cognition by bringing in the concept of the infinite and the infinitesimal, of beginnings and endings, of life and death, all for the sake of your wanderings in the domains of the endless Maya, endless perceived dualities.

For, in the dominion of Maya of dualities, all the particulars and the perspectives would crystallize into a perfect communion, a self-realization of reality, when the self-evident truth was embraced. In this self-realization, the world of Maya, of dualities, would disappear, and thus, all ills, all suffering, all disharmony would cease.

With the mind settled, and in peace, the physical world a perspective of a miraculous enchantment, the spirit in deep devotion of the creation and the creator, you were in self-evident bliss.

What followed next, physically, cognitively, spiritually, was a blissful celebration, an unfolding of a perspective of a miraculous reality in you and around you. Now the particulars of the unfolding reality would not be confusing or un-understandable but were reflections of the same miracle. One would blissfully cherish the miracle. One would be a part of the miracle, the miracle of creation.

Now you looked at the particulars, the so reflected particulars of reality, with a sense of a knowing. This knowing reveled in the awareness that all was a reflection of the same creation and the creator. It was all one and the same. There was no you, no it, you and it was all the one and the same creation. It became clear that the universe within you and the universe perceived to be outside you, was the same universe, the same creation. You understood the miracle. You were with your creator, and your creator with you, in you, all around you. That was the miracle.

In this enlightened self-realization, the particular you, blissfully smiled, inside and outside, and saw the same radiance in the reflections of reality. Reveling in this miracle, you, your reflection of you, in prayer and devotion, and in a bliss of knowing, continued your yatra. Thus, One was there, on this yatra trail, on this yatra, in a solemn reflection, a deep devotion, in a prayer, in a celebration of the creator and the re-creator of all.

On the yatra trail, now, a simple stone on the trail, a simple flower by the trail side, the sky above, the mountains all around, the breath that went into you, the breath that left you, were all reflections of the same miracle.

Thus, the particular you, the amalgam you, this you of observations and thoughts, and a spirit, this you, would revel in this miracle of reality, by its own particular reflections. That you, the physical you, the cognitive you, the spiritual you, was thus on this holy yatra trail to do a yatra, to be at the Holy Cave of Shri Amarnath Ji.

## Holy Śvetāśvatara Upanishad, Verse 4.10: Revelation

Herein, Verse 4.10 of the Holy Śvetāśvatara Upanishad became the object of meditation—revealing itself as both the realization and the lived reality of the Yatri on the Yatra Trail.

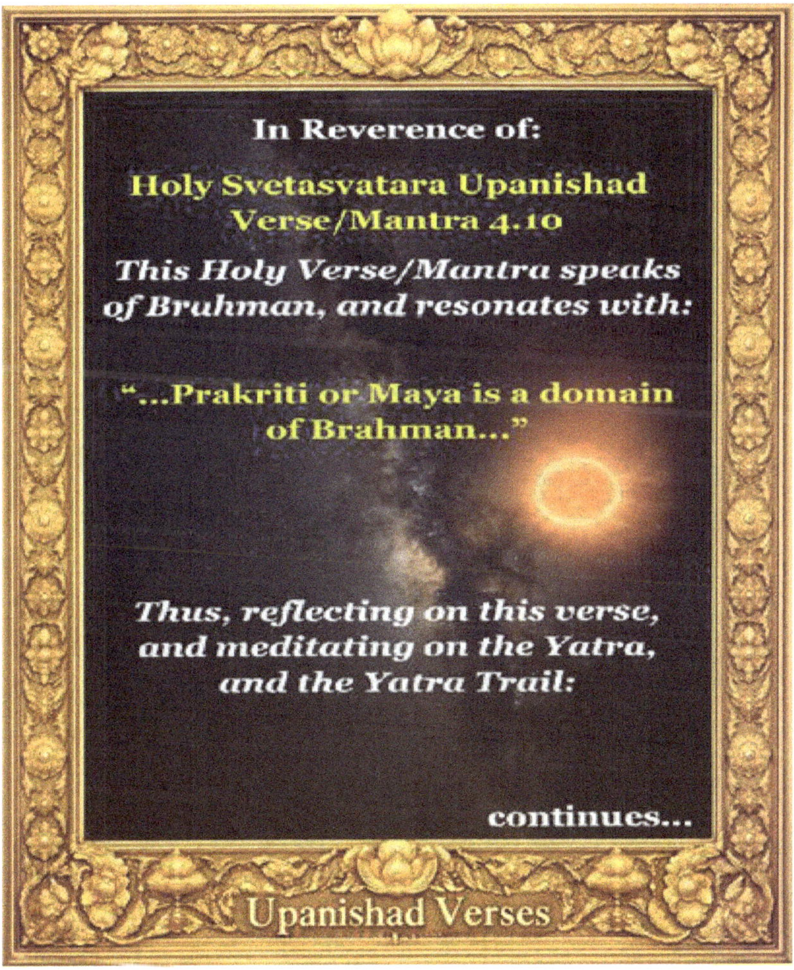

## Holy Śvetāśvatara Upanishad, Verse 4.10: Realizations on the Yatra Trail

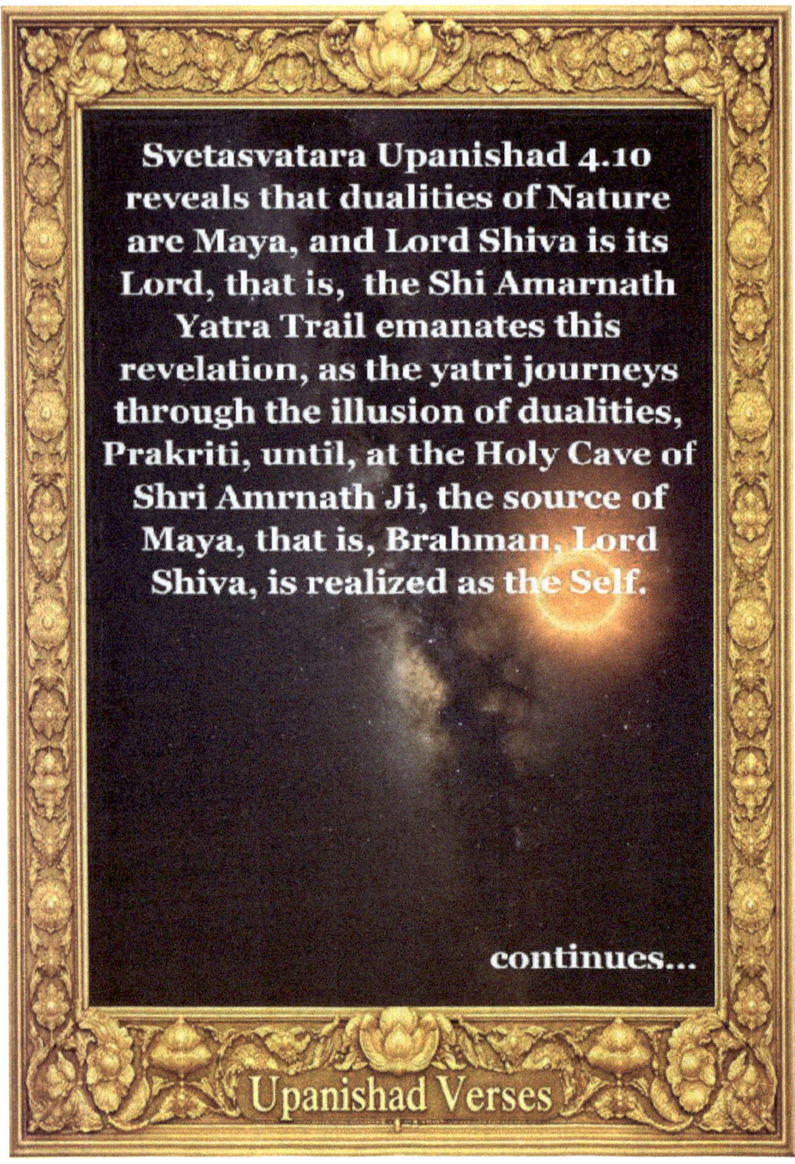

## Holy Śvetāśvatara Upanishad, Verse 4.10:
## Realizations on the Yatra Trail

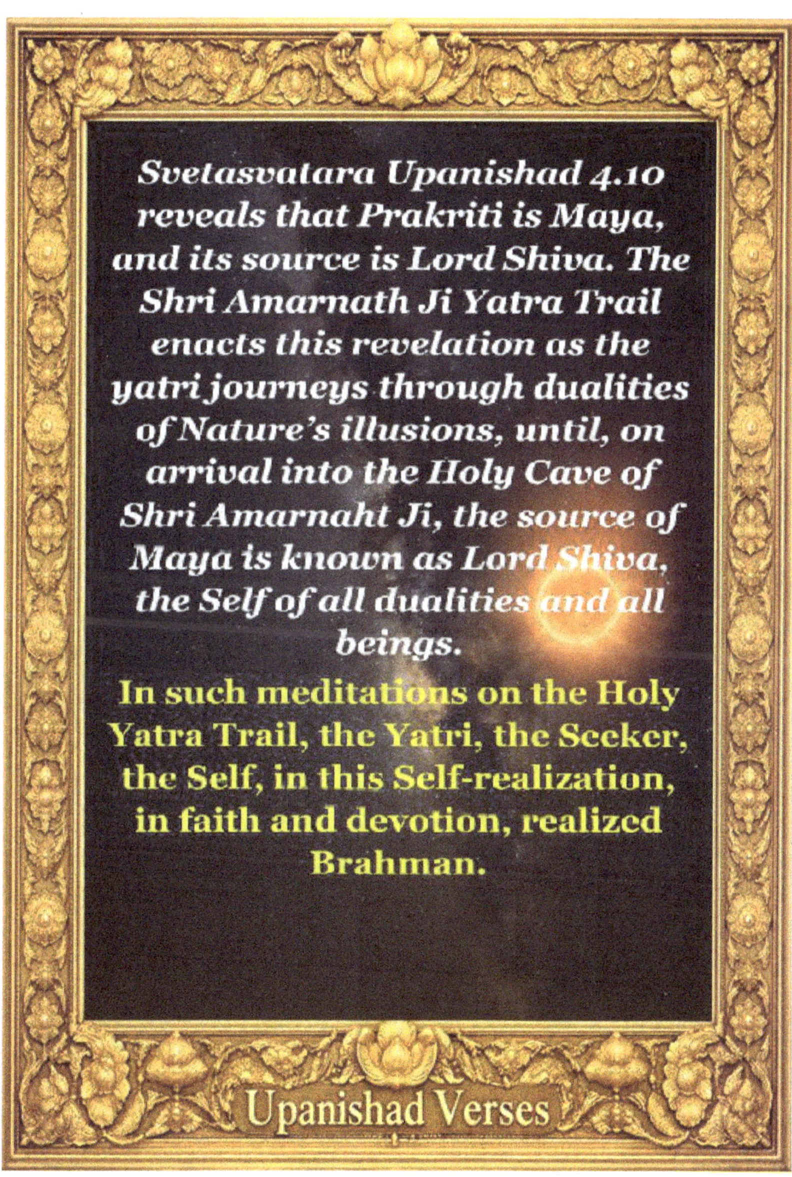

# PART FIVE: THE YATRA TRAIL ESSENTIAL TREKKING CONSIDERATIONS:

Important note to my contemporaries:

The information herein is based on a personal experience of a yatra conducted outside the main yatra period.

Please consider that the following suggestions, in this section of 'Preparing for the Yatra Trail Trek' are a result of a personal experience and provided herein as a personal perspective, that potentially, at least, provides for one perspective based on a historically contextual personal experience.

As such, the information herein is subjective and based on a historically time- framed personal experience.

Any authoritative information, at the time of the intended Holy Yatra must be obtained from the Government of India.

What follows herein are suggestions based a particular Yatra experience, and as such a historical perspective and a reference:

**Please remember that safety is your responsibility!**

Given the security concerns, the yatra administration rules, also, local weather and trail conditions: it is recommended that one should secure timely yatra information from the

Government of India Tourist Office in the preparation of the yatra.

Also, Government of India Tourist Office should be able to give you contact information of Travel-agents and organizations that can help facilitate your travel plans and arrangements for the Holy Yatra.

## EQUIPMENT CHECKLIST

Equipment Checklist/ some of the things you may need or want:

You or your guide/agent should provide the following items. Your travel-agent in India's major cities or abroad can provide you with a package deal, or you can link up directly with a travel-agent or trekking agency in Kashmir (Srinagar, Pahalgam, etc.). Remember, outside the main yatra period, **YOU WILL HAVE TO TAKE EVERYTHING THAT YOU NEED WITH YOU** (shelter, food, water, medicines . . . etc.).

During the main yatra period, which is in the month of Shravan (July-August), some arrangements for shelter, food, water, medicine . . . etc., may be available throughout the yatra trail. Again, at the time of the yatra, confirm these possibilities with the Government of India Tourist Office.

The list below is by no means exhaustive. This list should give you food-for-thought in the preparation of your own personal list. It is recommended that you consult with the Tourist Information Center at Pahalgam, as a last step affirmation of your preparation and readiness, before you begin your trek.

1. Tent, sleeping bags, sleeping-pads, ground-cloth: you or your agent.

2. Backpack: you or your agent.

3. Horses, mules and porter/guide: your agent.

4. Stove, fuel, pots, pans, food: you or your agent.

5. Clothing:

One must make provisions to potentially be caught in arctic like winter conditions (i.e., heavy snow, rain, winds) to potentially warm summer-like days. Such is the nature of high elevation mountain trekking.

Don't forget thermal-full-body-underwear, woolen head cap, raingear, parkas, etc. also for possible warm/hot afternoons, a cotton cap, light cotton clothes, small Towels (wipe away sweat, etc.).

6. Good hiking water-resistant boots and thick hiking socks.

You will be walking on all kinds of trail conditions.

7. Sunglasses & sunscreen.

A good pair of sunglasses is essential. In the rarified atmosphere found throughout the trail, the sun is sharp and bright. The sun reflecting off the snow on the trail and the peaks can cause severe strain on the eyes. Similarly, a sunscreen is also very important to protect your exposed skin from being sunburned.

8. Food and extra snack food:

High energy, complex carbohydrate types (dry-fruits (groundnuts, etc.), bread & Jam/Fruit-preserve, Biscuits, . . . etc.). If you can, an Insulated flask/Thermos for hot soup, or such, can be very useful. If possible, do visit your local sports or outdoors store for more suggestions on food and equipment. A Water-bottle is a must. Put some of these items in a small backpack and always carry it with you.

9. Water:

Take the amount of water that may be appropriate for the duration of the Yatra. Ask the local authorities in Pahalgam's tourist information center, at the time of the Yatra, about the availability of water along the trail. For drinking purposes, water collected along the way must be boiled or treated.

10. Fire-starter

Make sure you or your guides/cook has a way to get the stove started in possibly high winds, rain or snow conditions. (See your local sports/outdoors store).

11. Matches and waterproof-match-holder.

12. Medicines:

Your prescriptions and also Aspirin/etc for headaches, diarrhea medicine, cough-drops, cold-medicine, etc.

13. First-Aid kit

Moleskin (a thick flexible plastic adhesive medicinal tape) for blisters on feet, Band-Aids and gauze pads for cuts, antibiotic cream, thermometer, small scissors, etc. Put some of these in your small-back-pack that you always carry with you.

14. Chapstick/ skin moisturizer.

The dry and cold air in the mountain heights can very quickly dry up the lips, and exposed skin.

15. Personal articles: toilet-articles: biodegradable soap, small Towel, . . . etc.

16. Flashlight with extra batteries (a must).

17. Zippered plastic or other small plastic bags with Rubber-bands (for tying Bags): water-resist and seal and separate food, medicines, camera... etc.

18. Safety-pins, all-weather adhesive-tape, small piece of rope/cord (to patch up rips, tears, snaps, breaks, . . . etc.).

19. Camera.

20. A small notebook with your identification and the names, addresses and phone numbers of people that the authorities may contact in case of an emergency; always keep this on your person.

21. Maps for reference and general interest.

22. Notebook/journal:

If you like to keep a Journal; memories may fade; notes help.

23. Compass.

The trail is well defined, and it is almost impossible to stray from it. A compass would serve well as a tool to reference some of the features along the trail, just as a point of interest. More than that, there is no real need for a compass for the Yatra Trail.

24. Gloves.

25. Insect-repellent

26. Candles.

27. Pocket knife

One of those multi-feature ones: with can opener and bottle opener.

28. Staff/walking-stick.

A light and sturdy walking stick with a sharp point at its tip for crossing snow/ice fields and general support.

29. Small binoculars: for resolving the views, also, you can survey the trail conditions ahead.

## PHYSICAL CONDITIONING AND MEDICAL CONSIDERATIONS FOR THE TREKKER

Physical conditioning and medical considerations for the trekker:

The relative hazards of some areas of the trail is one of the fundamental reasons to traverse the trail only when one is well-rested and in good physical and mental shape.

When one is tired, the attention span diminishes and one's ability to concentrate is highly reduced. Under such conditions, chances of accidents are very likely. Such accident may result on a trail from mis-footing, or sudden wind gust while at the edge of a precipice, or just poor judgement. If one is well rested and in good shape, the unpredictable elements along the trail are more manageable. One must always approach the trail with respect and an attitude that promotes caution and discipline.

It cannot be overemphasized that careless actions or just unpreparedness in these Himalayan heights may not be recoverable. Periodic rest stops along the way with a frequent intake of proper nourishment will help in keeping a proper physical and mental disposition. Before you go, take a physical exam and also conduct vigorous walking exercises to get the legs and the heart in shape.

## TREKKING WITH MINIMUM IMPACT TO THE ENVIRONMENT

Trekking with minimum impact to the environment.

All of nature, and all the trails that open up the beauty and drama of nature, all across the planet, is a precious resource, to be passed intact from one generation to the next. It is each generations responsibility to safeguard this precious resource, as nature is a gift for each generation to behold. It is one's hope and concern that in our discovery of nature, nature should not suffer. There is a large system of trails in the Himalayas. There is a need to responsibly use such trails. Although the government, the local authorities, and to some degree nature itself, make a diligent effort to maintain and rejuvenate this entire network of trails, it is still an almost impossible effort to keep up with the effects of trail usage by thousands of people, year after year. These effects of trail damage range from trail litter to pollution of water sources, to general degradation of the local ecology.

Therefore, it really falls upon the trekker and the yatri to assume more and more of the responsibility of trail preservation and management, or else, we may over time loose this precious natural resource.

This philosophy of the trail users reducing their impact on the trail and the environment is being advocated world-wide by people and organizations who prize and respect nature as a precious and yet a delicate resource. This philosophy of guarded trail usage is often termed as "Minimum-impact" usage.

Shri Amarnath Ji Yatra Trail has been traversed for centuries. Over the recent past, the number of people on the yatra trail have numbered in the thousands in a given season. Such a large number of people on the yatra trail, season after season, requires "minimum-impact" usage of trail. Such a conservatory discipline is the only hope of leaving this precious Yatra Trail intact for our future generations. The following are some of the general conservatory guidelines, that is, Minimum-impact trail usage measures:

Prepare Appropriately and completely.

Follow local authorities' rules/guidelines.

Stay on the trail.

One should make every effort to keep to the Yatra Trail. This insures that the trails stay well contained. Meandering on and off the trail would cause erosion of the land along the trail. This, at the very least causes un-sightly tracks along the trail, and to the greater extent weakens the structural integrity of the trail.

Camp at designated sites.

Do not contaminate natural resources.

Do not introduce any contaminants of any sort into streams.

Adopt a no-fault policy of trekking: A no-fault policy of trail usage simply suggests that, when encountering any litter on the trail, one should try to remove it, regardless of the cause of the litter. As such, the Yatra Trail has a better chance to survive  the use by thousands of Yatris, trekker, year after year.

Om

Shanti

Shanti

Shantih

Peace within...
peace around...
peace from beyond...

Shanti

www.ingramcontent.com/pod-product-compliance
Lightning Source LLC
LaVergne TN
LVHW010602110826
845149LV00003B/735

*9798993019857*